Elementary School Science for the '90s

Susan Loucks-Horsley
Roxanne Kapitan
Maura O. Carlson
Paul J. Kuerbis
Richard C. Clark
G. Marge Nelle
Thomas P. Sachse
Emma Walton

The National Center for Improving Science Education
A partnership of The Network, Inc. and the
Biological Sciences Curriculum Study (BSCS)

The NETWORK Inc.
Andover, Massachusetts

Association for Supervision and Curriculum Development
Alexandria, Virginia

The work on which this publication is based was sponsored by the
U.S. Department of Education, Office of Educational Research and
Improvement, under grant number R168B80001. The content of this
publication does not necessarily reflect the views of the department or
any other agency of the U.S. government.

ASCD Publications present a variety of viewpoints. The views
expressed or implied in this publication are not necessarily official
positions of the Association.

Printed in the United States of America.
The type for this book was set using Xerox Ventura Publisher 2.0.

Printed by Automated Graphics System

Ronald S. Brandt, *Executive Editor*
Nancy Modrak, *Managing Editor, Books*
Lars Kongshem, *Editorial Assistant*
Al Way, *Manager, Design Services*
Stephanie Kenworthy, *Assistant Manager, Production Services*
Valerie Sprague, *Desktop Typesetter*

$13.95
ISBN: 0-87120-176-3
ASCD Stock No.: 611-90119

Library of Congress Cataloging-in-Publication Data

Elementary school science for the '90s / Susan Loucks-Horsley . . .
[et al.].
    p.   cm.
  "The National Center for Improving Science Education, a partnership
of the Network, Inc., and the Biological Sciences Curriculum Study
(BSCS)"
  Includes bibliographical references.
  ISBN 0-87120-176-3 (pbk.)
  1. Science—Study and teaching (Elementary)—United States.
I. Loucks-Horsley, Susan. II. Association for Supervision and
Curriculum Development. III. Network, Inc. IV. National Center for
Improving Science Education (U.S.) Biological Sciences Curriculum
Study.

LB1585.3.E43   1990
372.3'5'0973—dc20   90-47016
                                          CIP

Elementary School Science for the '90s

Foreword v

Acknowledgments vii

Introduction ix

1. Make Science a Basic 1

2. Build Curriculums that Nurture
   Conceptual Understanding 14

3. Connect Science to Technology 27

4. Include Scientific Attitudes and Skills
   as Important Goals 40

5. View Science Learning from a
   Constructivist Perspective 47

6. Use a Constructivist-Oriented Instructional
   Model to Guide Learning 58

7. Assess What Is Valued 72

8. Connect Curriculum, Instruction,
   and Assessment 81

9. Use a Variety of Assessment Strategies 92

10. Assess Programs as well as Students 108

11. View Teacher Development as a
    Continuous Process 120

12. Choose Effective Approaches to
    Staff Development 130

13. Provide Teachers with Adequate Support to
    Implement Good Science Programs 141

Appendix A. 159
General Reference List for Science Leaders

Appendix B. 161
Science Resources

About the Authors 165

Foreword

As any 1st grade teacher will attest, *all* youngsters entering their classes in September have bright shining eyes and an eagerness to unlock the secrets of their universe—to understand the science of how the world works. Teachers play a major role in sustaining that sparkle by feeding the wonder of their young charges. Unfortunately, far too many twinkles are snuffed out before the middle/junior high school years.

Many teachers are uncomfortable with their level of science teaching expertise, and, for many, teaching science is not a high priority. Whether teachers lack knowledge of content or teaching methods, the result is the same: U.S. students are less science literate than many of their counterparts abroad.

Research statistics have substantiated that the number of students coming through the educational pipeline adequately prepared for higher levels of science is declining. Black and Hispanic students, though showing interest in the early years and making strides in most other basics, are noticeably absent from secondary and collegiate scientific curriculums. Females, too, are not keeping up in numbers with their male counterparts in science. With an increasing dependence on women and minorities in the work force, continuing along this path will be devastating to our nation and to the individuals whose opportunities have been cut off.

Our science-deficient curriculums are effectively disqualifying the United States from contributing to the worldwide search for scientific and technological solutions and further reducing our economic power. In fact, with the increasing quality-of-life issues facing us today, such as environmental pollution and world hunger, to stay the course is to act as a lamb being led to slaughter.

Recognizing our dilemma, President Bush has provided this nation with direction by establishing a national goal related to science preparedness. His priority is to "make American students first in the world in math and science achievement by the year 2000."

Bush's words, however, are empty without a plan of action. The authors of this text have provided that plan of action. Teachers, administrators, school boards, and communities at large can ignite a perpetual flame in the minds of youngsters by heeding these words.

DONNA JEAN CARTER
ASCD President, 1990-91

Acknowledgments

IT MAY COME AS A SURPRISE TO THE READER THAT, IN A BOOK WITH SO many authors, there would be others who made significant contributions. But that is indeed the case. A book that purports to be rich in resources must itself draw on a wide variety of resources to achieve its goals.

Among those we wish to thank are David Kennedy, Science Supervisor for the state of Washington, and Martin Brooks, Assistant Superintendent of the Shoreham-Wading River (New York) Public Schools, who fine-tuned our manuscript for relevance and usefulness. We appreciate the input and support of the Center's 15-member advisory board, and the 16 members of our three study panels whose reports provided the material for this book. The contributions of many science educators who took time to talk with us and provide useful materials about their programs are also appreciated. And we especially thank Senta Raizen and Audrey Champagne, the Center's directors, and Rodger Bybee, Chair of our Curriculum Panel and Associate Director of BSCS, for their ongoing critiques and useful additions to the book.

Our production team moved the effort from a collection of good material to a readable book. We thank Don Horsley for his detailed and able editing, Denise Cartwright and Clif Lund-Rollins for their patient and careful word processing, and Lori Larsen and John Fleener for keeping the communications between authors moving and productive.

THE AUTHORS

Introduction

- Will the earth still have an ozone layer in the year 2020?
- Will Americans continue to eat too much and exercise too little, cutting their lives shorter than they need to be?
- Will workers in the year 2000 have the thinking and reasoning skills they need to succeed in their jobs?
- Will our great-grandchildren live in a world where half the species we know now are extinct?

SCIENCE AND SCIENCE LEARNING ARE POPULAR MEDIA TOPICS TODAY. More and more, citizens are making decisions through actions (and inactions) that affect their own lives and those of others—decisions that require some measure of scientific literacy. Many of those decisions are sending us down paths toward lives that are less rich in the resources, health, opportunities, and freedoms that we now enjoy. Fortunately, most of those paths are not one way; we still can do much to maintain and even enhance the quality of life on our planet. Two important things we can do are to pay more attention to science and to provide children with the right kinds of opportunities to learn it. The purpose of this book is to help educators create opportunities for elementary school children to start on the road to scientific literacy.

We need to ensure that science is an important part of children's educational experience. Besides helping them make better life-long decisions about themselves and their world, science promotes critical thinking. *More than a body of knowledge, science is a way of thinking.* It helps children develop skills in observing, developing explanations, reasoning, and making informed decisions. Valuable in and of itself, science also reinforces other programs of study, such as language arts, math, and social studies.

The time is right for promoting science in schools. With more and more interest in science learning, there are lots of success stories. Many teachers, schools, museums, curriculum developers, national associations, and states are launching bold experiments to improve opportunities to learn science.

Yet many others have had neither the resources nor the opportunities to address children's science learning needs, or they see the barriers to progress as too steep. They are plagued, and sometimes paralyzed, by an endless list of questions:

- Where do we start?
- What should kids learn?
- What changes will make the most difference?
- How can we manage all the materials and the mess?
- How do children really learn best?
- How will we know we're succeeding?
- Where do we get the resources?
- How can we motivate teachers?
- How do we convince people that science is important?

This past year, the National Center for Improving Science Education, convinced that children need an early start, has taken an extensive look at science in the elementary years. We identified and synthesized the answers given by research, recent reports, and practical experience to the overarching question, "What is good science education, and how can it be ensured for every child?" What we learned is discussed in a series of reports listed later in this chapter. What we found that is most useful to practicing educators—people who ask the questions listed above—is included in this book.

WHO IS THIS BOOK FOR?

This book is for decision makers: people who have or share responsibility for school and district science programs. While some of you hold the formal title of science supervisor or coordinator, many have no specific science background and have other priorities in addition to science—roles such as assistant superintendent, curriculum coordinator, principal, and lead teacher. We also address this book to those of you with statewide responsibility for science, with the hope that you will find it a useful way to share good strategies for science programs with others in your states.

WHY IS THIS A GOOD TIME?

There are a number of reasons why this is an especially good time for science education, and, thus, for science leaders to improve children's opportunities for early science learning. First, science education is getting a great deal of attention, although most of it is not positive. International comparisons, as well as examinations of science learning within our country, indicate that students of all ages are not learning science (International Association for the Evaluation of Educational Achievement 1988, Mullis and Jenkins 1988). Leaders from business and industry have voiced strong concerns about how ill prepared their employees are to tackle the jobs available today, let alone jobs of the future (Scheuer 1987, Twentieth Century Fund 1983).

Such attention has been motivating. It has caused many who have not been concerned about science, or for whom science has not been a priority, to take notice and, in some cases, action. While the movement in state legislatures to increase graduation requirements has not reached down into elementary schools, the message is clear: Children must be better prepared than they are now. Some states are clarifying their goals for science in the early grades, providing impetus for new and better approaches to science teaching. Movements toward reforming teacher education and restructuring schools to enhance student learning have the potential for positively affecting science education. And there is experimentation with making tests and assessments correspond to improved science curriculums. This is critical, since what gets tested usually gets taught.

Current attention to science education is different from what followed the launch of Sputnik in the late 1950s. Now the move is toward science for *all*, not science for only those who would be scientists. We are talking now about general scientific literacy, with attention to population groups currently touched in only limited ways by science: women and minorities. While increasing our country's supply of scientists is still important, equally if not more important is the need to raise the general level of scientific literacy for *all* people. This is necessary if people are to make informed decisions about major issues that face us and our world, issues like nuclear power, personal health, the environment, and reproduction. The fact that these issues are reported and debated daily bolsters the case for attention to science education.

A final reason why it's a good time to focus on science education is that we now know a lot about how to improve school programs. The '60s and '70s science program development efforts left some excellent materials, and we now have better understandings of where and how they can be used. New curriculum development will soon offer options for schools that combine new materials and teaching strategies with staff development and support systems for teachers. Most elementary schools and teachers have subscribed to the idea of activity-based science, although more aspire to using it than are actually doing so. New cognitive research suggests some additional strategies for turning what is often just "hands-on" science into "minds-on" science as well. Further, the literature on staff development and school change offers a variety of effective approaches to addressing the need to nurture the development of people as well as programs and to providing the support needed to sustain initiatives for improving science education over time.

HOW CAN THIS BOOK BE HELPFUL?

The messages, the motivation, the momentum—all seem pointed in the direction of addressing science learning needs of children. But where do we start? How can we get a handle on all that needs to be done and all we need to know to do it?

This book addresses these questions. It is organized by 13 findings of the National Center's work on elementary school science (Figure 1), and is worded and directed as recommendations to science leaders. Except for the first recommendation, they are organized to respond to questions about *curriculum* (What should we teach?), *instruction* (How should we teach?), *assessment* (How can we identify successful learning?), and *teacher development and support* (How can we prepare and support teachers to teach science well?).

A chapter is devoted to each of the 13 recommendations. For each we discuss:

• What is known from research, literature, and practical experience;
• What can be done?

Figure 1
Findings of the National Center for Improving Science Education

1. Make science a basic.

Curriculum: What Should We Teach?

2. Build curriculums that nurture conceptual understanding.
3. Connect science to technology.
4. Include scientific attitudes and skills as important goals.

Instruction: How Should We Teach?

5. View science learning from a constructivist perspective.
6. Use a constructivist-oriented instructional model to guide learning.

Assessment: How Can We Identify Successful Learning?

7. Assess what is valued.
8. Connect curriculum, instruction, and assessment.
9. Use a variety of assessment strategies.
10. Assess programs as well as students.

Teacher Development and Support: How Can We Prepare and Support Teachers to Teach Science Well?

11. View teacher development as a continuous process.
12. Choose effective approaches to staff development.
13. Provide teachers with adequate support to implement good science programs.

- Roles that can be played by local and state science leaders, both short-term and long-term;
  - Resources, materials, and exemplary programs; and
  - Key references.

Appendix A contains a list of basic references, a "must have" selection for anyone interested in science education. Appendix B provides contact information for the resources, models, and exemplary programs described in the text. Throughout the book we have included examples, checklists, and suggestions for illustration and motivation. There is no one way to pursue program improvement, but knowledge of these important components, an assessment of where one is currently, and a willingness to experiment are good places to start.

Additional Reports from the National Center for Improving Science Education

In the Center's first year, the following reports on elementary school science were completed:

• *Science and Technology Education for the Elementary Years: Frameworks for Curriculum and Instruction*
• *Assessment in Elementary School Science Education*
• *Developing and Supporting Teachers for Elementary School Science Education*
• A concise synthesis of the three reports, written for a broad audience: *Getting Started in Science: A Blueprint for Elementary School Science Education*

These reports provide substantial details on each recommendation in this guidebook, in addition to specific references to research and the literature on science education. Similar series of reports, focused on middle school science and secondary school science, are forthcoming.

WHAT DOES GOOD ELEMENTARY SCHOOL SCIENCE TEACHING LOOK LIKE?

Good elementary school science teaching engages children in the wonder and the study of the natural world. It makes links to technology—the ways human beings have solved problems and adapted to living in the world. Science gives children opportunities to explore how things work firsthand, through activities and experiences with a wide variety of materials. It stimulates them to wonder, to be good observers, to make predictions, and to offer explanations. It helps them construct their own knowledge of scientific principles and concepts, making these part of the way they see the world and the decisions they make about their lives.

We choose to call this approach to science education "constructivist science," for reasons that will become clearer in later chapters (especially Chapter 5). It's not enough to call it "hands-on science" or "activity-based science," since children can easily be engaged in hands-on activities with no attempt to help them derive meaning from their experiences. They are either left on their own, or they are told what they should have observed or learned. Constructivist science is based on the notion that we learn best when we are able to construct our own knowledge. Helping children do this from real-life experiences is good science teaching.

The following vignette illustrates what constructivist science looks like in practice.

"How do seeds live? Can seeds grow way, way deep in the ocean and make seaweed?" "How do seeds get inside of watermelons?" "Hey! How do they make watermelons without seeds in them?" "How do seeds grow plants?" These were some of the many questions asked by Ms. Lopez's 2nd graders. Today they are thinking about seeds, the topic they are about to study, and Ms. Lopez is keeping track of these questions on a chart entitled "Questions We Have About Seeds." Another chart, entitled "What We Know About Seeds," is filled with such statements as "seeds grow in parks and gardens," "you can eat sunflower seeds," and "carrots don't have seeds." These charts are referred to time and time again as Ms. Lopez encourages questions to help the children develop concepts and change opinions. She uses the children's questions and comments to decide that the class is ready for a "seed walk."

This morning the students go to a nearby park to collect seeds. Each child, besides carrying a collection bag, wears an adult sock pulled up to the knee over one shoe, providing a fuzzy surface to which seeds can cling. When the children return from the walk, they select one seed to study carefully with a hand lens. After each child makes observations about what the seed looks, feels, and smells like, and guesses how it might have traveled, the child makes a presentation to the class in a meeting circle. Ms. Lopez keeps track of the kinds of seeds discussed by taping the specimens onto a chart. After the children tally the kinds and numbers of seeds collected by the class, they develop picture graphs of the results.

That evening, Ms. Lopez reflects on the differences in the children's understandings of the structure and function of seeds. She notes which children easily made observations and which ones had more difficulty, which groups made more obvious or more unexpected responses, which children seemed comfortable using the lens for examining their seeds, and which ones seemed more awkward. As she thinks of the multiple activities for the next day, Ms. Lopez uses her notes to place children in groups so that their discussions will prompt and challenge one another's inquiry.

The next day, some groups count the seeds on their socks and then plant them in large plastic bags, watering and setting them in the window area. In the days that follow, they will be encouraged to observe the germination process carefully and to compare the total number of seeds with the number that sprouted by making "ratio" sentences. Ms. Lopez invites other groups to compare the size of seeds by outlining the seeds on graph paper and then counting the number of graph squares each seed covers. The students discover a great diversity of sizes and shapes in different kinds of seeds, and that the same kind of seed has variations in size and shape. Still other groups choose to continue working in the "seed journals" that Ms. Lopez requires all students to keep. They are either to paste in or draw the specimen and then write about three seeds of their choice, including the same type of observations they shared earlier in their meeting circle. Since students of this age have a range of sentence-writing capabilities, Ms. Lopez meets with each child to discuss his or her observations and writing. She uses the journals and evidence from the meetings to monitor the level of understanding the children have of such concepts as diversity and cycles.

Ms. Lopez's class spends most of the week working on this science topic, incorporating writing and math with inquiry-based science activities. Other activities she will do with the children include a fiction story about how a native American girl uses seeds and plants, a garden song, and drawing the seedlings as they grow. Her thematic, active learning approach is similar to one she observed and practiced during her first year as a teacher, when she was coached by a mentor as she tried her first interdisciplinary unit.

In successive lessons, Ms. Lopez calls groups together and, based on their explorations, asks several questions. As she records the responses, Ms. Lopez asks the children to clarify their answers. Eventually, she will introduce new vocabulary information that will help the students reflect on their developing concepts. Some of the children may not be sure about the new information; they will need more time to talk about it, and they will do some additional testing of their ideas to help make the new information part of their personal understanding of seeds. When Ms. Lopez taught this unit last year, for example, several youngsters insisted that the lima bean embryos they discovered earlier would grow into lima bean plants even without the seed halves attached. They were convinced that the embryos could "eat" the soil and water and grow into adult lima bean plants. Through careful questioning, Ms. Lopez was able to guide these children to design a test of their beliefs. She found that they changed their point of view after they conducted the investigation, and that they now had some additional questions to pursue.

After several weeks of studying seeds, Ms. Lopez recognizes that the children have learned a great deal about such science concepts as diversity, life cycles, and structure and function. They have become adept observers and ask questions of each other and of her concerning these developing concepts. Ms. Lopez knows they will soon be ready to apply these new levels of knowledge and skills to other science areas. The children will, as a group, construct a booklet on how to plant seeds and care for the seedlings. Ms. Lopez will keep notes on the progress of individual students and the class as a whole. This will help her plan and design more effective science instruction to use in future classes. It will also provide source material that will enable her to make more formal assessments in report cards, in conferences with parents, and—for the class as a whole—to Mr. Sandowski, the 3rd grade teacher.

Ms. Lopez's choices of curriculum, model of learning, and modes of assessment are all discussed in detail in the chapters that follow.

References

International Association for the Evaluation of Educational Achievement. (1988). *Science Achievement in Seventeen Countries: A Preliminary Report.* Elmsford, N.Y.: Pergamon Press.

Mullis, I. V. S., and L. B. Jenkins. (1988). *The Science Report Card: Elements of Risk and Recovery.* Princeton, N.J.: National Assessment for Educational Progress, Educational Testing Service.

Scheuer, J. H. (October 1987). "Competitiveness and the Quality of the American Workforce." Opening statement, hearings before the Subcommittee on Education and Health of the Joint Economic Committee, United States Congress, Washington, D.C.

Twentieth Century Fund. (1983). *Report of the Twentieth Century Fund Task Force on Federal Elementary and Secondary Education Policy.* New York: The Twentieth Century Fund.

1.
Make Science a Basic

Although only 5 percent of the current student population will choose a scientific career, *all* students will live in a world that is increasingly shaped by science and technology. Science capabilities will be required for individual decision making and for the economic and technological advantage of our country. Making science a priority in schools today can equip students to live in the complex world of tomorrow.

WHAT WE KNOW

Until recently, science education has not been considered basic in the elementary program. Consequently, it has not received the attention and support at either the national or state level to build the types of strong networks and implementation mechanisms characteristic of reading and mathematics programs. The most effective program models to date exist outside the United States in countries like Japan, the United Kingdom, Hungary, Germany, and Israel. One favorable outcome of the hail of negative reports of poor U.S. student performance in science is the attention now focused on the improvement of science education, especially at the elementary level. The renewed interest in science as basic is evident in the funding the National Science Foundation now receives and directs toward improving science education programs across the nation.

Though a spotlight is now on science education, some educators remain skeptical and persist in asking, "Why make science a priority in elementary schools?" There are many reasons; following are several of the most important:

We know, for example, that an important prefix to producing scientifically literate adults is actively involving kids in doing science when they are young. Observe children at play and you will undoubtedly agree that they *want* to know about the fascinating world in which they live and to share what they're learning with others. Kids are born scientists—just listen to the questions they ask about the beauty and wonder of the earth and the technological wizardry that continues to transform this planet.

It is equally important to recognize that **science education prepares students for what lies ahead as well as furthering the basic goals of education.** All students will face major challenges when they leave school: They'll need to become fully active voting citizens, secure jobs in an increasingly competitive world, and make capable plans and choices based on available information. Good science education addresses these needs in countless ways. Consider, for example, how problem-solving skills learned in science can help a person to make thoughtful decisions about the costs and benefits of protecting the environment while living in an expanding world economy. Or how students may one day compete in the international marketplace for a growing number of jobs requiring technical and managerial skills well beyond what most high school graduates exhibit today.

As consumers, and perhaps as parents too, students will have to make difficult decisions about the role technology will play in their daily lives. And, as lifestyle choices play an increasingly important role in health, people will need to make informed decisions about how to get and stay healthy. **Clearly, knowledge of science and technology can move students in significant ways toward achieving all the goals of education while at the same time helping our nation to seize the obvious economic and technological advantages of scientific literacy.**

How can we ensure that students take advantage of what science education has to offer? First, we need to make time for science in the elementary curriculum. **Students need to spend far more time than they are now spending in the related fields of science, technology, environmental education, and health** to cull the substantial advantage from solid, science-related learning. Ideally this would happen from kindergarten through grade six, and not just when teachers happen to have a good science unit.

Second, we need to seriously address the fact that science is not seen as a basic for *all* students. Many researchers, and even the public, are finally taking note of the coursework, career choices, and the low scientific literacy of many females and minority high school students. When given a choice, they tend to steer clear of science. This "turn off" to science generally occurs in the middle grades, so it may be that elementary schools somehow fail to turn kids on to science, especially females and minorities. Solving this problem will require more than a scorecard and superficial, quick fixes. Rather, we must work to make and keep science a priority in elementary schools by using meaningful science learning to capture and maintain the innate curiosity of all students throughout the elementary grades. In this way, no one will be left out of the thrust toward more technical sophistication.

Finally, let's keep in mind that **by setting the stage for good science learning, teachers play a pivotal role** in helping students discover for themselves how the world around them works. When teachers work to sustain this curiosity through the middle grades, students are more apt to feel positive about continuing to learn science.

If teachers can play a major role in facilitating true science learning, why then do most not give science education the "basic" status it deserves? Simply because teachers understandably teach what they are most comfortable with, and since little of their preparation and inservice training focuses on helping them become competent science educators, we cannot realistically expect them to feel good about teaching science. A description of Chris Zajac, a second grade teacher whose classroom life is portrayed in Tracy Kidder's (1989) book, *Among Schoolchildren*, says it all:

> She left science for last. For several other subjects she used textbooks, but only as outlines. She taught science right out of the book; this was one of those texts that takes pains with the obvious and gives the complex short shrift. Chris didn't know much science and didn't usually enjoy teaching it. Sometimes she let creative writing encroach on science's time. About one day in ten she canceled science altogether and announced—to cheers, Felipe's the loudest—an informal art lesson. She often felt guilty about science (p. 32).

Chris Zajac is not alone. Science is rarely taught at the elementary level, and when it is taught, it's often at the end of a long school day. The absence of substantive training also helps to perpetuate the myth among some elementary teachers that teaching science is hard, and that they may not be smart enough to pull it off.

Another reason that science is not yet a basic is that, even when given the opportunity, many teachers opt not to upgrade their skills in science education—and why should they? In the current system, there are few incentives to do so; administrators at all levels do not see science as a priority. And there are few if any rewards for teaching science well, compared with those for exemplary language arts and math teaching.

It is therefore clear that **without sufficient training, knowledge, and materials, teachers will not change their minds or their practices regarding science education.** To make science genuinely basic, teachers must be provided with the necessary academic background and decision-making opportunities to choose appropriate curriculum materials and classroom methodologies. A quality science education program has students actively engaged in science learning. Fortunately, most teachers already have the zest for learning and teaching techniques that can help children learn by experience—the cornerstones of excellence in science teaching.

Although there are clear benefits from employing basic scientific and technological thinking skills, we as a society will not be able to realize them unless we do a better job of giving science education the priority it deserves.

TAKING ACTION ON WHAT WE KNOW

How can we make science a basic? We can start by creating a clear and public need for science education by marketing the benefits of a comprehensive elementary science program. Grab both staff and community interest by making science something *everyone* can do and benefit from—kids, teachers, parents, the school, and the community—by providing learning experiences that excite people and convince them that learning science is useful and can have direct application to their daily lives. Such activities might include science olympiads, Family Science (science activities for parents and kids to do together after school), Saturday academies, and taking advantage of museums, zoos, and botanical gardens. Promotional events need to spell out the benefits of learning science, including increasing the base of scientific literacy for all, acknowledging the marketability of science learning, keeping America economically competitive through technological and scientific advantages, and fostering the overall goals of education by preparing students to make knowledgeable decisions about the environment, their health, and other science and technology issues they face daily.

Another way of making science a basic is to **use it as a vehicle to teach critical thinking skills.** What better way to learn to analyze, reason, ask questions, and test ideas than through experiences with scientific phenomena. These skills can then be applied throughout the curriculum.

Formulating a comprehensive vision of science education for the state or district would also help to make science a basic. This effort begins by developing a philosophical basis for the program that is founded on both a school and community vision. Current policies, like time allocation, could then be reviewed for their enabling capacity. Other "vision efforts" might include adopting effective teaching strategies, like the instructional model proposed in this book, and allocating resources for (1) teacher and leadership development, (2) materials that support good science education, and (3) a comprehensive assessment system that is based on the learner outcomes sought by the new program.

The issue of classroom time is central to making science a basic. **To be adequately prepared to become scientifically literate, students need to spend between 120 minutes (in grades K-3) and 300 minutes (in grades 4-6) per week on science and technology education.** Currently, elementary students spend about as much time in science as they do in spelling: roughly 100 minutes per week. This amount falls far short of what it takes to achieve scientific literacy. And it's not just a matter of *how much* time is spent on science, but of *how* that time is spent. Science education that is worth the investment of time is characterized in Chapters 2 through 4.

Many educators wonder, "How can I find time to teach science given the already crowded elementary curriculum?" Our answer is to integrate other school subjects with science in appropriate ways, thus using science experiences to teach other basics. Indeed, language arts instruction would be enhanced by the substance of science as subjects for reading and writing, and the real problems generated by science questions could be used as a vehicle for learning math. It is important, though, to guard against losing the integrity of the discipline at hand during the process of subject integration, taking care not to use one content area merely to illustrate another. Instructing students to draw leaves with crayons, for example, does not make for an integrated art-science lesson. What then constitutes a useful approach to subject integration? Employing the same example, students could observe different leaf types, and subsequently draw serrated, lobed, and notched leaves. In this way, the concept of diversity would be explored. While integration of subjects is desirable, it is not the panacea for reaching the recommended time allocations, or for making science a basic. Other strategies are considered at various points in this book.

LOCAL ROLES

Things to do now:

1. Initiate a public relations campaign that spells out the benefits of a solid science program. Principals, teachers, and science supervisors can illustrate the value of successful science programs at PTA, PTO, and back-to-school programs as well as to community groups, local newspapers, and cable stations (see Figure 1.1). Feature science education along with reading and math, so that parents and the media develop an expectation for achievement, homework, and extracurricular activities like field trips and science clubs. This will create a positive cycle, wherein the public requests information about science programs and educators regularly provide the "hot news."

Figure 1.1
Ideas for Media Coverage

- Requests for citizens to serve on science curriculum review committees, which get a pool of interested community members involved and signal to the public that curriculum is being reviewed.

- Reports by committee members of their experiences, what they learned, and what their opinions are of the course to be taken in curriculum review.

- Letters to the editor by committee members to share positive experiences.

- Reports of what is being done locally, prepared and released following major national news stories (e.g., comparison of test scores, Department of Education pronouncements).

- Articles in university publications describing how faculty and staff members aid science education projects, stressing collaborative efforts supported by national research. This aids and strengthens all institutions seeking community support.

- "Grabbers" that will interest the media, like kids' pictures and unique activities, can explain what educators are doing in developing, revising, or implementing a new science program. In one community, for example, isopod (rolly polly) behavior was being studied in a school district science unit. Isopod races at noon at the city center involved business as well as school teams. The event was sponsored by the Audubon Society's Urban Education Program, developed as a community complement to the school district's curriculum development process.

2. **Identify or develop exemplary science programs that meet the district's vision of what science education ought to be.** Then support program adoption with appropriate training, resource allocation, and other considerations that will ensure successful implementation.

3. **Provide incentives that recognize the achievements of principals and teachers** who, despite the myriad of obstacles, are involved in developing and maintaining exemplary science programs. Incentives can include educational bonuses funded from state, federal, or private sources; trips to national or regional

meetings of professional associations; or special roles as science specialists, trainers, or resource people.

4. Establish communication and lines of authority between district curriculum leaders and other program staff, such as Chapter 1 and special education. When administrators, teachers, and parents do not see science as a basic, it is easy to justify pulling students out of science class for special help in language and math. Yet science can be particularly useful by helping students unsuccessful in other areas to learn language and math by exploring and making sense of their natural world. Further, because Chapter 1 and special education students are disproportionately minority students, who, as they grow up, participate less and less in science, it is particularly important that these students participate fully in elementary science programs. Categorical program staff at all levels need to work more closely with science curriculum staff to diminish the negative attitudes and science anxiety that obstruct scientific literacy for all. Seeing that no children are pulled out of science class for special assistance and including categorical program teachers and aides in science inservice programs can go far in establishing science as a basic.

A "can do" attitude will accomplish more for science education than either money or mandates.

Things to do for the future:

1. **As new assessments are developed, publish the results and celebrate the outcomes.**

2. **Encourage extracurricular programs** like Invent America!, Family Science, and science olympiads, which highlight student involvement and promote science awareness in the community. Look to sources of informal science education, such as museums, zoos, and parks. Link school efforts with those of local scientists as well.

3. **Develop liaisons** with community leaders, representatives from the business community, and state and federal agencies to

reinforce science as basic to the elementary curriculum. Ultimately, education in America is a grass-roots enterprise. Despite the rhetoric of top-down control, teachers and schools remain the locus of control in this large and complex system. State and federal policies will value the will of the teaching community if a consensus forms around science as basic; in turn, this will pave the way for creating "science-as-basic" initiatives.

4. Include science on the agendas of staff meetings, district reviews, and as a specific part of building goals. District administrators can regularly check with building administrators, asking, "How is the science program going in your building? Have you heard the kids talking about it? What are teachers saying about it? Have you had any reaction from parents?" Likewise, building administrators can ask teachers, "How is science going? What's the most exciting thing your children learned in science recently? How much time are you spending on science? What are parents saying?" This type of ongoing attention will help reinforce the belief that science is important.

STATE ROLES

> The most important function that a state agency can play is to keep science in the policy arena.

Things to do now:

1. Designate science assessment results as a priority, along with reading and mathematics scores (but only if and when the assessment is a good measure of valued science learning outcomes). Each year, major press releases focus on performance in the three Rs. If science were added to that tracking, principals, school boards, superintendents, parents, and teachers would pay closer attention to the quality of their K-6 science program. Chapters 7 through 10 include strategies for measuring "learnings that count" in science education.

2. **Identify praiseworthy elementary science teachers and programs** in the state, and feature them as models for other schools and districts to emulate. Recognition programs, like a governor's award for excellence in science teaching, serve the dual function of keeping success in science in the public eye and rewarding elementary teachers for their accomplishments.

3. **Begin a statewide elementary science initiative that trains elementary teachers** in how to use their vast repertoire of experiential learning techniques in the context of science and technology education. The campaign should showcase the enormous payoff to teachers applying their skills to promote new kinds of learning.

4. **Send a strong message to categorical program leaders and teachers to promote science as a basic** for students in Chapter 1 and special education programs. Not only is science an important motivating vehicle for teaching other basic subjects, but emphasizing science in elementary grades may alleviate the lack of interest in science of minority students in later grades.

5. **Acknowledge that science is basic** by advocating appropriate levels of classroom time, inservice opportunities, and instructional material funds. Providing money, mandates, and classroom time to make science education a basic sends a message throughout the education community about the priority that science in schools deserves.

Things to do for the future:

1. **Sponsor an annual statewide Science for the Elementary School Conference.** Feature teachers and others who support the kind of science described in this book. Invite school people as well as those from universities and intermediate agencies whose role it is to support the continuous learning of teachers and the implementation of new programs in schools.

2. **Promote science education as doable for every district and school in the state.** Adding science as a basic will not succeed if it is perceived as an onerous task. A science education effort must build from a base of local support that has created long-term maintenance of reading, writing, and mathematics programs.

3. **Begin a long-term public relations campaign** to help parents and community leaders value science education as a priority. The campaign plays on three important themes: (1) the

economic prosperity (new and expanding job markets) and enhanced quality of life that are an outgrowth of scientific literacy; (2) the enjoyment and self-confidence that develop in people who have a command of their place in the natural and technological environment; and (3) the teaching of critical thinking skills, so necessary for future learning and decision making.

4. Work through professional associations, such as those for math and reading, to identify strategies whereby science education can be promoted and described as essential. The important point to emphasize in cross-curricular discussions is the need to preserve the valued outcomes for each subject. The science needs to be accurate, the mathematics need to be correct, and the grammar needs to be conventional in integrated tasks.

5. Develop incentive programs for districts and schools that create and maintain exemplary elementary science programs for all students. Beyond simple recognition, districts and schools where science excels need to be viewed as models and rewarded. Take advantage of these settings by appropriating funds to use them as professional development centers that provide special assistance to schools in surrounding areas.

6. Implement a system of review for all districts, and define sanctions for districts that fail to adhere to state standards for the quantity and quality of science programs at the elementary level. As a last-ditch strategy, it may become necessary to pressure districts that will not or cannot offer their students a basic science program. Productive forms of correction involve assistance, mandates, and permanent staffing; external inoculations of the quick-fix variety, like one-time inservices, will be useless in the long run.

MODELS AND RESOURCES

A Local Model: The purpose of the Denver Audubon Society Urban Education Dissemination Project is to develop and support knowledgeable community members who understand and advocate an effective school science program. The project's manual and personal assistance guide community members to provide leadership, obtain funding, and offer meaningful training to adult volunteers for delivering a learning program in ecology for 3rd through 5th graders in urban settings. Similar projects are run by local Audubon Societies in Seattle, Wash., Prescott, Ariz., Arlington, Tex., Louisville, Ky., and Boston, Mass. In Birmingham, Ala., the Ruffner Mountain Nature Center takes the lead, and in

Broward County, Fla., the local school district and PTA are the sponsors.

A Local Resource: Family Science, under development by the Urban Coalition, offers a set of activities that parents can use with their elementary-aged children outside of the school day.

A Local Resource: Invent America! is a national education program and student invention competition designed to stimulate creativity and develop problem-solving skills. Available to all public and private school students in grades K-8, Invent America! culminates in an annual national competition in Washington, D.C., with student inventors who have won competitions in their schools, states, and regions. The program is sponsored by the United States Patent Model Foundation.

A Media Resource: *A Private Universe*, a film developed by the National Astrophysics Center at Harvard University, underscores and illustrates the misconceptions adults hold about scientific concepts, even after they have completed many years of formal education. Distributed by Pyramid Films and Media.

A State Model: *The New York Elementary Science Syllabus* is an example of an effort to make science a basic part of the elementary school curriculum. First, it stipulates that science is as basic as language arts, mathematics, and social studies. It makes clear that scientific literacy must begin early with regular, positive experiences with the natural world. Second, it acknowledges the role of basic thinking abilities in the development of the whole child. It shows how facility with numbers and words is absolutely necessary to the development of scientific concepts. Third, it recognizes the wider contribution science can make to developing a broad range of intellectual skills for all children. The syllabus demonstrates the manner in which youngsters learn how to learn via the methods of science.

Note: Contact information for models and resources in all chapters can be found in Appendix B.

Key References

American Association for the Advancement of Science. (1989). *Science for All Americans*. Washington, D.C.: AAAS.

Bybee, R. W. (1986). "The Sisyphean Question in Science Education: What Should the Scientifically and Technologically Literate Person Know, Value, and Do?" In *Science-Technology-Society*, 1985 Yearbook of the National Science Teachers Association. Washington, D.C.: NSTA.

Champagne, A. B., B. E. Lovitts, and B. J. Callinger, eds. (1989). *This Year in School Science 1989: Scientific Literacy*. Washington, D.C.: American Association for the Advancement of Science.

Daedalus. (Spring 1983). Special issue on scientific literacy.

Harlen, W., ed. (1985). *Primary Science: Taking the Plunge*. Portsmouth, N.H.: Heinemann.

The Harvard Education Letter. (May/June 1990). "When Kids Do Science." 6, 3: 1-5.

Hurd, P. D. (January 1986). "Prospects for the Reform of Science Education." *Phi Delta Kappan* 67: 353-358.

Kidder, T. (1989). *Among Schoolchildren*. Boston: Houghton Mifflin.

McCormick, K. (June 1989). "Battling Scientific Illiteracy: Educators Seek Consensus, Action on Needed Reforms." *ASCD Curriculum Update*.

National Science Board Commission on Precollege Education in Mathematics, Science and Technology. (1983). *Educating Americans for the 21st Century*. Washington, D.C.: NSB.

Yankelovich, D. (1984). "Science and the Public Process: Why the Gap Must Close." *Issues in Science and Technology* 1, 1: 6-12.

2.
Build Curriculums that Nurture Conceptual Understanding

Effective elementary science programs incorporate major scientific concepts and themes into study topics of interest to children. In doing so, they help children function well in the bewildering complexity of the natural world.

WHAT WE KNOW

In Chapter 1 we answer the question, "Why make science a basic?" In this chapter, and in Chapters 3 and 4, we address the question, "What should be taught in the science curriculum?" The conceptual approaches we advocate stand in stark contrast to typical approaches to elementary science, which emphasize discrete topics, uncoordinated facts, and disembodied vocabulary. These only reinforce the complexity of the natural world, rather than giving children powerful conceptual tools that can help them make sense of nature's complexity.

Most teachers orient their programs around topics, focusing on the factual information associated with each. But a "topics with the facts to match" approach to science curriculum works only if the chosen topics and their attendant facts illustrate concepts that pervade science and technology. When children learn the importance of patterns and how to find them, they have the knowledge and tools to begin simplifying and understanding a complex world. In a similar fashion, other "big ideas" provide frameworks for understanding the richness and complexity of science and technology. Here's why:

For starters, **free-floating, out-of-context facts are generally meaningless to most—if not all—students.** This is especially true for young students and those whose learning styles are visual, tactile, or holistic, rather than symbolic. Vocabulary-driven curriculum guides and textbooks often result in science classes that resemble trivia games. Is this the kind of science learning we want for young people? Will it provide them with meaningful information that is relevant to our time in history, as well as students' own lives and cultures? And, finally, does it have a useful purpose?

We don't think so. Instead, children need to develop an understanding of a few major concepts that explain how the world around them works.

Children invent concepts on their own. Good science programs help them do so more effectively by creating rich environments that encourage exploration and concept development. In this way, children develop conceptual understanding as they construct and refine concepts that integrate their experiences into coherent wholes.

> Science education should give life to the popular aphorism, "less is more."

The examples that follow illustrate how conceptual approaches to elementary science contribute to the development and application of powerful science concepts. Dinosaurs and seeds are two of the most popular topics in the elementary science curriculum. As these topics are usually taught, the focus is on factual information and scientific vocabulary. Children memorize the names of the dinosaurs; they learn which were the largest, which were plant eaters, and which had bony projections along their backbones. This vocabulary-laden, factual approach to dinosaurs misses opportunities to introduce concepts that are easily developed while studying dinosaurs, such as *diversity* and *variation*.

On the basis of appearance, dinosaurs and seeds have little in common. Dinosaurs are animals; seeds are parts of plants. Dinosaurs are extinct; seeds are capable of developing into living organisms. Despite their differences, each can be used to illustrate concepts that apply across the biological sciences. As students engage in the study of these organisms, they have the opportunity to refine ideas they have invented to organize the natural world and to learn how these ideas apply to natural objects that would seem to have little in common.

Through the activities of collecting and sorting seeds and dinosaur models, students learn about diversity and variation in biological organisms. Dinosaurs and seeds exist in diverse sizes and shapes. Some species of dinosaur are hundreds of times the size of a third grader, while others could be easily carried under the same third grader's arm. But not every Tyrannosaurus Rex was exactly the same size. Just as humans vary considerably in height, Tyrannosaurus Rex varied in length. In a similar fashion, observations of a collection of seeds or the measurement of the lengths of lima beans illustrate the concepts of diversity and variation.

When students sort dinosaurs and seeds on the basis of physical attributes, they are learning to impose *order on their natural environment and to search for relationships between an organism's structure* and the ways in which it *functions*. For instance, dinosaurs can be sorted by the shape of their teeth: We know that dinosaurs with flat teeth were plant eaters while those with pointed teeth ate other animals. Thus the *form* of the teeth can be related to the *function* they serve, namely grinding plant materials or tearing animal flesh.

Seeds also illustrate the pervasive relationship between form and function, something Ms. Lopez was well aware of as she planned her lesson (see Introduction, pp. xv-xvii). Her students sorted seeds based on the characteristics of their seed coats. Seeds that caught on students' socks as they shuffled through the weeds have hooks on their seed coats that catch on clothing or animals and are carried far away from the parent plant. Seeds that are left behind have smooth seed coats. Some are thick, indigestible, and are dispersed by animals in their feces. Other seeds are aerodynamic; they are dispersed by being shot out of dried seed pods or have wings that carry them along on the breeze.

Children's investigations of the solar system contribute to the development of other concepts: *system, model, scale,* and *change.*

As children learn about the position of the planets relative to each other and to the sun, they come to realize structural relationships among the components of a larger system. Building scale models of the solar system contributes new meaning to the concept *model* and a new dimension to the meaning of *scale*. Observations of the moon over a period of several months gives enriched meaning to the concept *change*. These same observations contribute to the idea of systematic changes that are repetitive. Thus the phases of the moon provide children with an example of a *cycle*, a concept that occurs again and again in the natural world.

Scientific concepts such as *diversity, variation, order, structure, function, model, scale, system, subsystem*, and *change* integrate topics as diverse as dinosaurs, seeds, batteries and bulbs, and the solar system. A conceptual approach to science consciously draws children's attention to these concepts as they study different aspects of the world around them.

Conceptual approaches make sense. Concepts bring *coherence to the natural world* and unite the scientific disciplines. Concepts provide a framework for elementary science curriculums, which students can use to integrate facts and experiences. They promote greater understanding from fewer topics, through depth rather than breadth.

Concepts bring coherence to information and experience. Free-floating, out-of-context facts and vocabulary are meaningless and are remembered only until the end-of-chapter test. Science classes that resemble training grounds for trivia competitions are a waste of time.

Concepts enable lifelong learning. Facts are important, but concepts are more powerful learning tools. With experience, children elaborate on and increase the sophistication of their concepts; comparatively simple understanding of a concept such as cause and effect is adequate to most situations children encounter. But more important, children begin to build from their childhood experiences, continuing to elaborate their concepts into the more sophisticated understandings required to deal effectively with issues of adult life.

The approach we advocate is consistent with recommendations of scientific and mathematics groups. For example, new national standards developed by the National Council of Teachers of Mathematics (1989) state:

A conceptual approach enables children to acquire clear and stable concepts by constructing meanings in the context of physical situations and allows mathematical abstractions to emerge from empirical experience. A strong conceptual framework also provides anchoring for skill acquisition (p. 17).

While the organizing concepts differ from report to report, their basic importance is recognized by all. For instance, the American Association for the Advancement of Science's (1989) Project 2061, named for the year Halley's Comet will once again visit us, is a national effort to define what the well-educated citizen should know in that year. Project 2061 identifies six common themes that pervade science, mathematics, and technology: *systems*; *models* (including physical, conceptual, and mathematical); *constancy* (including stability and equilibrium, conservation, and symmetry); *patterns of change* (including trends, cycles, and chaos); *evolution* (including possibilities, rates, and interactions); and *scale*. The Project 2061 authors argue that science curriculums should be centered around these themes because the themes appear repeatedly throughout the history of humankind and they transcend disciplinary boundaries.

In a fashion similar to our recommendations and those of Project 2061, the California State Department of Education (1989) urges curriculum developers and teachers to weave six major overarching themes into the science curriculum: *energy, evolution, patterns of change, stability, systems and interactions*, and *scale and structure*. The California authors recognize that alternative themes or major concepts might be used, provided that they permit integration of otherwise isolated facts and minor concepts. A curriculum that has a thematic structure allows students to see the connection of facts and concepts across the scientific disciplines.

For the first time in recent educational history, several significant educational groups, working independently, have recommended that the way to achieve a curriculum that emphasizes depth over breadth is to highlight major ideas, concepts, or themes, rather than masses of detailed terminology and facts. But what does this growing national consensus mean for developing curriculum? Are we calling for a common scope and sequence centered around just a few themes? Is it appropriate to develop units of study for each of the identified themes or organizing concepts? We don't think so.

> If we want science curriculums to have lasting value for students, we must address the "big ideas" so that detailed information about science becomes connected, becomes meaningful, and contributes to successful problem solving.

Curriculums can be organized in several ways. Some are organized around topics of interest to children; some are organized around the processes of science; some adapt materials already in hand to match important new learning goals in science; still others, indeed, are organized around major concepts. Regardless of where curriculum developers start, we suggest that they look for ways to illustrate or reinforce a set of major concepts throughout the elementary years.

As we have shown, teachers need not discard such favorite topics as dinosaurs and batteries and bulbs. Rather, they can treat existing units in ways that will nurture conceptual development. For instance, dinosaur study lends itself naturally to the idea of scale and the use of models. Through the activities of observing, measuring, and inferring, these important concepts will be enriched in the minds of students who are captivated by dinosaurs and want to learn more about them.

Batteries and bulbs are commonly found in elementary science programs. They are appealing to children; use common, readily available materials; and can be used to create an environment that nurtures the development of concepts, skills, and attitudes of science. "Can you make the bulb light using one battery, one bulb, and one wire?" invites students to engage in exploration. In the course of their investigation, they will question, hypothesize, make predictions, test their ideas, fail, try again, design experiments, formulate models, and interpret data. They will make decisions. They will become acquainted with another example of cause and effect, change, a system (the simple circuit), and making models. The conceptual approach differs substantially from one that teaches the single "right way" to light a bulb or requires memorizing technical terms such as conductor, resistance, ampere, and volt.

Major concepts can also provide a framework for curriculum developers designing new units of study. Ms. Lopez chose to teach seeds for a variety of reasons: They were interesting to her students, they were in the children's natural environment, and they were an important building block of plants—key elements of the natural world. Ms. Lopez could have designed a seeds unit that was fun and followed the children's interests but wouldn't necessarily build conceptual understanding. Instead, she also considered major ideas that could be incorporated into the unit. As she designed the unit of study, she selected activities that encouraged her 2nd graders to use their study of seeds to help them refine their understanding of such concepts as diversity (Are all seeds alike?), scale (Do big plants come from small seeds?), and change (What is the life cycle of a flowering plant?). While sophisticated understanding of these concepts is not expected for 2nd graders, the experiences of elementary science are essential to their development.

This orientation provides a "connectedness" that also fosters scientific "habits of mind" and a positive attitude about learning science, as children witness experiments and participate directly in activities that fit into some larger picture.

TAKING ACTION ON WHAT WE KNOW

What steps will help schools create elementary science curriculums that nurture conceptual understanding?

First, science leaders at all levels should alert the profession and the public to the need for a more thoughtful, conceptually rich curriculum for all students. Fortunately, many organizations like AAAS, NSTA, and the National Center are already issuing statements for more concepts and fewer details. They can use the work of these organizations in presenting this new thinking to practitioners and the public. It is equally important for universities, states, and districts to work together in the movement toward depth over breadth. Curriculum guidelines, syllabi, and college entrance requirements must be modified to develop a more holistic, concept-oriented approach to science learning.

Next, we need to ask what current textbooks and other instructional materials emphasize. What do they highlight in their bold, underlined, or shaded text: facts, terminology, and minor concepts; or major concepts, skills, and themes? Most likely the former. What do the questions they ask students call for: understanding or rote memorization? We need to apply these questions to elementary science kits, laboratory manuals, and such educational technology as microcomputer simulations and interactive videodiscs. No one material or set of materials will cover all pertinent concepts, skills, and themes; supplementary materials must be found to round out the curriculum so that by the time they reach high school, students will have had lots of experience with a range of important concepts.

> It is inappropriate to blame commercial publishers for textbooks that do not reflect what we know about good science education. It is *our* role to create the demand for instructional materials that stress depth over breadth—in states where adoptions exist, and in districts throughout the country.

A third area we need to examine is assessment. Do our assessment systems focus on concepts, themes, and skills that cut across topics? For formal assessment, clearly we need to move from test items that reward only convergent thinking to assessment tools that tap students' abilities to be divergent thinkers who can explore multiple concepts and connections. Hands-on and performance assessment strategies need to be developed that provide insights into what parts of science concepts are understood and how they were learned. This is as true for assessments used by the teacher in the classroom as it is for wide-scale assessments mandated by a district or state.

Informal instructional activities can also heighten student understanding of concepts, themes, and skills—science olympiads, exploratorium-type museums, and other avenues for students to share their experiences in the broader educational community. Clearly, both formal and informal science learning will need to mutually reinforce a depth-over-breadth approach.

LOCAL ROLES

Things to do now:

1. **Meet with instructional leaders to analyze existing curriculums** to see how the materials can be strengthened to develop conceptual understanding. Use big ideas that weave through science activities and are reinforced across grade levels.

2. **Create mechanisms for the selection of text and instructional materials** that are consistent with this approach. Curriculum coordinators and staff can assess texts and materials for what they highlight, what types of skills and understandings are called

for by student questions and activities, and what outcomes are stressed.

3. **Reward individual students and cooperative learning teams that master divergent thinking** rather than convergent thinking related to trivial science facts.

Things to do for the future:

1. **Provide staff development opportunities** that emphasize depth of scientific understanding over isolated, unconnected information. A useful method might be to walk teachers through a sample curriculum or unit of study that builds depth using major concepts, themes, and skills, and then ask them to examine their own program's topics in a similar way.

2. **Base selection of new teachers** (and current teachers' professional development plans), **in part, on their orientation** toward such strategies as:

- Teaching that incorporates major concepts of science (e.g., cause and effect, organization) rather than merely focusing on interesting but unconnected informational content;

- Informally assessing the prior knowledge that children bring to the science topic at hand, so that the teacher can make judgments about where to begin and how certain activities might help children link new knowledge to what they already understand;

- Using textbooks in a way that encourages children to link new knowledge to prior knowledge so they develop a more refined understanding of major scientific concepts;

- Using assessment and grading practices that reward students for struggling to understand new concepts rather than only reciting textbook information.

3. **Bring both parents and community into the classroom** to experience a concept-rich, depth-over-breadth approach to science education. Encourage community-based efforts (e.g., museums, science fairs, science olympiads) to take this same approach.

STATE ROLES

Things to do now:

1. **Encourage and promote dialogue among curriculum leaders**, including science supervisors and building principals, to forge a professional consensus on the importance of conceptual development to elementary science instruction. Building principals are critical change agents, so they need to understand the importance and significance of the big idea orientation. Moreover, this view needs to emanate from a consensus among curriculum leaders across districts.

2. **Encourage university science educators and academic department faculty** to join elementary educators in fleshing out when and how major concepts, themes, and skills can be emphasized within topics that are appropriate, or are traditionally taught, in the elementary grades. Changing to this approach is a challenging task that requires content specialists and practitioners to join together to design a few high-quality units of study—units that focus on a topic like seeds, but which include activities that allow kids time to wrestle with major conceptual understandings.

3. **Develop and disseminate curriculum guides and other documents that provide models of how major concepts and themes can be used in learning science.** The National Center's report, *Science and Technology Education for the Elementary Years: Frameworks for Curriculum and Instruction* (Bybee et al. 1989), provides insight into this approach. Units of study developed in Item 2, above, can be collated and shared at state and regional professional association meetings.

Things to do for the future:

1. **Develop and disseminate inservice programs** that serve as models of how districts can implement a concept-rich approach to science instruction. Models should help teachers see how they might design lessons, use cooperative learning strategies, use textbooks to develop conceptual understanding in children, ask effective questions, and assess student learning of concepts rather than isolated facts.

2. **Encourage colleges, universities, and school district personnel departments** to develop and nurture preservice pro-

grams that emphasize teaching for big ideas. Changes will be necessary in the science courses prospective teachers take as well as in professional science curriculum and instruction courses. Curriculum guides and other documents developed in response to item three, above, could be used to strengthen these emerging programs.

3. **Develop textbook adoption standards** that favor textbooks that incorporate major concepts, themes, and skills. These differ from the typical perspective, which results in coverage of multiple content domains and extensive lists of new science vocabulary.

4. **Work closely with assessment personnel and test companies** to encourage the development of assessment procedures and instruments that focus more on major conceptual understandings and problem solving, rather than mere recall of verbally learned concepts, names, and definitions of terms.

MODELS AND RESOURCES

A National Model: The model proposed by the AAAS—Project 2061—was discussed earlier in this chapter. The report, *Science for All Americans*, outlines in detail a set of major organizing themes that curriculum developers can incorporate into their instructional materials. In the second phase of Project 2061, six school districts are developing curriculum prototypes that reflect this approach to learning science, mathematics, and technology.

A Model Curriculum: The Education Development Corporation (EDC) is also developing a new K-6 curriculum in science, Improving Urban Elementary Science. The curriculum will include a series of modules that encourage children to investigate a problem or topic in depth. The curriculum is aimed at children in urban settings.

A Model Curriculum: The Biological Sciences Curriculum Study (BSCS) is developing a new K-6 curriculum in science, health, and technology that is organized around major concepts. The curriculum includes instructional approaches that encourage children to link new knowledge to prior knowledge and develop a strong understanding of fewer ideas rather than a shallow understanding of many.

A Model Curriculum: The Life Lab Science Program is being designed to expand on a program that has been in existence for more than ten years and that integrates conceptual learning and practical applications. The program functions mainly around a garden, involving students in hands-on experiences with materials that are both affordable and manageable.

A Model Curriculum: The Full Option Science System (FOSS), currently under development by the Lawrence Hall of Science, builds science concepts for students in grades 3-6 through the use of multisensory, laboratory-based science activities.

A Model Curriculum: The National Science Resources Center (NSRC) is currently developing *Science and Technology for Children*, a collection of 24 science teaching units for grades 1-6 on topics in physical science, life science, earth science, and technology. In the units, children work with hands-on materials to explore scientific phenomena and thereby learn both scientific concepts and science process skills.

State Models: Several states have or are developing curriculum guides and other documents that emphasize teaching science for conceptual understanding. These include the State Science Framework in California, the Elementary Science Syllabus in New York, and similar documents in Oregon and Tennessee.

Local Models: Many innovative school districts—including Accord, New York; Minneapolis, Minnesota; Mesa, Arizona; Anchorage, Alaska; and Schaumburg, Illinois—have assembled instructional units and materials that address significant science concepts or themes at the elementary level.

In Accord, New York, for example, a Roundout Valley School District elementary school created a hybrid program that combined units of study from its adopted commercial textbook series and the state science syllabus. Teachers selected their favorite units, which were then screened by a science mentor. The mentor, a staff member at a regional service center familiar with elementary teaching and the state syllabus, then compared the units to the state framework and designed new units that addressed gaps. Revisions were made based on teacher feedback. The mentor arranged workshops on units for which teachers felt they needed additional training.

Key References

American Association for the Advancement of Science. (1989). *Science for All Americans*. Washington, D.C.: AAAS.

Bybee, R. W., C. E. Buchwald, L. S. Crissman, D. Heil, P. J. Kuerbis, C. Matsumoto, and J. D. McInerney. (1989). *Science and Technology*

Education for the Elementary Years: Frameworks for Curriculum and Instruction. Andover, Mass.: The National Center for Improving Science Education, The NETWORK, Inc.

California State Department of Education. (November 1989). *Science Framework for California Public Schools*. Pre-publication draft. Sacramento, Calif.: CSDE.

National Council of Teachers of Mathematics. (1989). *Curriculum and Evaluation Standards for Mathematics*. Reston, Va.: NCTM.

New York State Department of Education. (1985). *Elementary Science Syllabus*. Albany: The University of the State of New York.

Sachse, T. (November 1989). "Making Science Happen." *Educational Leadership* 47,3: 18-21.

3.
Connect Science
To Technology

Finding out where mountains come from and developing a way to travel around them are pursuits of science and technology, respectively. The study of science proposes explanations for "what is" in the natural world, whereas the study of technology provides solutions to human problems of adaptation. They go together like hand in glove and will have a mounting impact on our social and personal environment.

WHAT WE KNOW

In this chapter we consider the issue of helping students learn both science and technology. In linking the two, we are talking about more than just teaching *with* technology (e.g., using microcomputers); we're talking of teaching *about* technology.

New technological advances continue to change our understanding of the world at an alarming rate. Students need to be prepared to cope with the mounting effects of both science and technology on their own lives and on society as a whole. How useful is science education if we only teach students to define fusion and fission and don't prepare them to vote responsibly on the proliferation of nuclear power sources? Is it sufficient for citizens to be able to complete a Punnett Square, or is it better that they be able to understand the risks and benefits of releasing a genetically engineered bacteria into a field of strawberries? These examples reflect our expectations for scientifically and technologically literate adults, and the foundations of that literacy must be built in the elementary years.

In their early years, children are surrounded by technology, or at least the hardware of it: Big Wheels, skateboards, flushing toilets, light switches, ballpoint pens, flashlights, and school buses. But other aspects of technology are also part of their lives: public transportation systems and the design of neighborhoods and even entire cities. Second graders can productively spend time designing a simple city on an area of their classroom floor. Where should the McDonald's go? the dump? the hospital? the residential areas? the industrial areas? the schools? Integrating science and technology allows kids to explore in even greater depth the big ideas—systems, for example—that we described in Chapter 2.

We can begin to move in a productive direction by employing an integrated approach to learning science and technology. Technology education is every bit as important as science education. Like science, a technological thread weaves through the very fiber of our lives by influencing such arenas as medicine, transportation, communication, and agriculture. Technology education aims to provide students with ways of *dealing with* the complexity of modern life. The focus of science education, on the other hand, is to encourage students to *propose explanations* for observations about the natural world.

> Technology education demonstrates both human and scientific responses to complex problem solving and can benefit students by giving them a deeper understanding of how technology affects their daily lives.

What then would an effort to connect science to technology education look like? Reading about the technology introduced by Thomas Edison is *not* an example of science and technology education; it could lead to it, however, if we expand the effort to engage students in meaningful activities like designing and conducting experiments to test which of many possible filaments would make the brightest, longest lasting light bulb. Additional activities can push students to determine, for example, the safest, most cost-effective light bulb. The former activities are more in the realm of pure science and reflect commonly known methods of inquiry. The latter activities are more in the realm of technology, for they reflect the application of problem-solving and decision-making strategies rather than scientific methods of inquiry. But, frankly, it is difficult to separate science from technology. And while we can do it intellectually, in practice—particularly in the early grades—the two are inextricably intertwined.

Learning with microcomputers and other electronic media does not reflect an integrated approach to science and technology education. The use of educational technology to enhance teaching and learning is often confused with technology education. But technology is more than hardware. Our definition views technology as more than hardware and the manufacture of that hardware, more than applied science, and more than a method or system.

Technology originates in problems of human adaptation to the environment and goes on to propose solutions to those problems. It is only by linking science to technology that we facilitate meaningful learning within these two rapidly advancing fields. Figure 3.1 illustrates the relationship between science and technology.

Science and technology education does not currently occupy a significant place in the elementary school program. **But if we agree with the need to connect science to technology, we must start to explore ways to incorporate them into an elementary program, for it is important to begin learning at an early age how science and technology are intertwined.** We suggest that some of the science time in elementary grades be spent on making purposeful connections between science and technology. We should spend time on issues, on uncovering the science and technology behind those issues, and on inventions—devices and machines—and the science underlying them.

A typical issue might be air pollution. Here, children can begin with a straightforward question: What is pollution? This can lead to other questions such as, What are the causes of pollution? Is invisible pollution (e.g., carbon monoxide) acceptable? How much pollution are we willing to live with? Can we clean up the air by banning private automobile transportation and mandating mass transit? What are the costs, risks, and benefits of doing so?

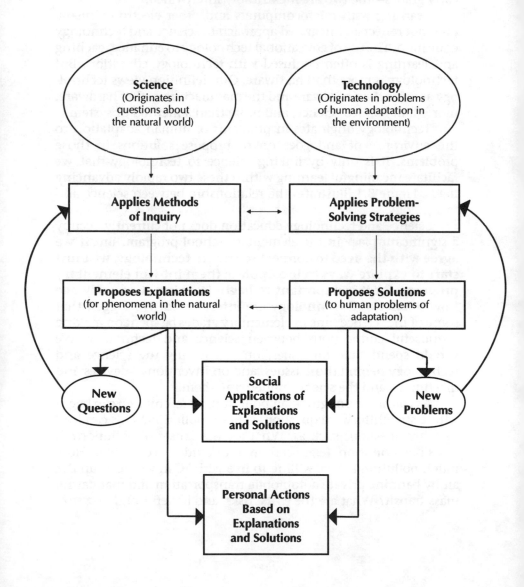

**Figure 3.1
The Relationships between Science
and Technology and their Connection
to Educational Goals**

As children begin to search for answers to these scientific and technologic questions, they uncover a wealth of information on the science part of the problem. They also delve into the technological side. All the while, they are participating in the kind of science we described in Chapter 2: a major concepts approach. In this case, they are learning about systems and subsystems and cause and effect, to mention just two major themes.

The issue of pollution is a societal problem and is an example of what science educators refer to as a "science-technology-society" (S/T/S) approach to the curriculum. But not all of science and technology are directly related to societal issues. For example, children might wish to investigate the science and technology behind a mountain bike. To better understand the decision-making process of a bike's designer, one has to begin to wrestle with the physics behind the bike. Why does a mountain bike typically have 18 speeds instead of the 10 or 12 speeds characteristic of a touring or city bike? For what type of terrain would you want a very knobby tire? A less knobby tire? Again, questions like these help the students develop an understanding of major scientific and technologic themes like structure and function. Of course, a teacher could extend this example into the societal arena by having the children address questions about when and where mountain bikes should and should not be used. For example, should we ban the use of mountain bikes in ecologically delicate areas?

Successfully linking science and technology education also enhances the development of thinking processes, including essential information-gathering skills (e.g., observing, inferring, experimenting), problem-solving skills, and decision-making skills. Currently, most elementary science programs focus on students' acquisition of science informational knowledge. This pattern promotes the presentation of rotely learned content, like identifying parts of a flower or naming the components of an electrical circuit. Rarely are children challenged to use their thinking skills by investigating how the parts of a flower might function together or exploring how a flashlight works and how an inoperable one might be repaired.

The wonderful benefit of combining science and technology is that deep content—understanding systems, for example—is uncovered, information-gathering processes are practiced, and the higher order processes such as problem solving and decision making emerge in what can become lively sessions that begin to prepare children for a world that is becoming increasingly complex. Rather than creating artificial dichotomies between science and technology or process and content, we should help students discover these fields of study as the integrated whole they really are.

How much of the normally allotted time for science should be spent on technology? Because we are recommending an integrated science and technology curriculum, we can only say that all the time currently allocated to science should be devoted to the new science and technology approach.

We know from Chapter 2 that it is both possible and desirable to teach fewer concepts more deeply. Following this model will allow ample time to introduce and examine the interaction of science with technology in a way that students find compelling. In addition, students will have more time for both science and technology as these subjects are sensibly integrated with basic and advanced skills in reading, writing, and mathematics. We are, therefore, recommending a new kind of literacy—one that assures students' acquisition of basic literacy and their acquisition of science and technology literacy as well.

When students learn more about the development of new technology, they gain an understanding of the processes by which scientific and technological advancements occur. Students at an early age really do grasp concepts such as constraints, tradeoffs, risks, and cost effectiveness; they learn these ideas as consumers of treats, entertainment, and other items. In fact, students who learn about the everyday aspects of science and technology are eager to understand more about their complex technological and natural world. As Paul Hurd (1986), professor emeritus of science education from Stanford University, sagely advises, "The thinking processes typical of technological problems closely parallel those that individuals use to solve personal and social problems occurring in everyday life."

Children's early experiences with science and technology should enhance their curiosity about the natural and technological world, help them to develop an understanding and appreciation for the limits and possibilities of science and technology, and contribute to their ability to act responsibly in the conduct of human affairs.

Taking Action On What We Know

What can you do to further the connection between science and technology education in your school, district, or state? Begin by incorporating curriculums and instructional materials that explore both science and technology, as well as those curriculums that explore the complex interrelationships among science, technology, and society (S/T/S), and make them part of the core science curriculum. An outgrowth of the acceptance, refinement, and expansion of the science and technology education movement has been the proliferation of a new crop of curriculums and instructional materials. Most often these materials remain supplemental to the core (textbook) program.

Since many S/T/S materials treat controversial issues such as nuclear power, global warming, contraceptive devices, and genetic engineering, they are not routinely brought into the classroom, especially at the elementary level. But is it not time to go beyond the technology of simple machines and batteries and bulbs? If it's acceptable for students to spend five hours a day—more than 1,800 hours a year—in front of a television set, then surely they can spend a week or two in school finding out how the technology they pay homage to works; how television programming affects society at large; and, perhaps most important, what high-quality endeavors they give up when they choose to watch an electronic hypnotic instead of playing tag, building a model, or reading quality prose.

It bears repeating that a strong step in the direction toward linking science to technology is to *allocate all of the allotted science time to science and technology education.* Some national reports, like AAAS's (1989) *Science for All Americans,* and state guides like New York's *Science, Technology, and Society Syllabus,* already exist as models of curriculum direction. States and districts would benefit by moving toward alignment with this growing professional consensus of more time for technology. Clearly, state and local school boards will need to be involved in the approval of such changes. Also, their endorsements of the curriculum guides will signal acceptance for classroom-level implementation of potentially more complex and controversial science teaching subjects that also link to societal issues.

We need to capitalize on teachable moments that afford us unique opportunities to focus on issues or problems that are science and technology-laced. The earthquakes in northern California, Hurricane Hugo in South Carolina, and the Exxon oil spill in Alaska are examples. The first two are natural events that become devastatingly important because humans have used their ingenuity and technology to build where early humans couldn't—on the outer barrier islands of the Carolinas and the former mud flats of San Francisco's Marina district. Oil spill problems can be natural—fissures in the earth's crust can appear spontaneously—but, clearly, an oil spill from a ship is a human-caused, technology-based problem.

All of these incidents provide marvelous moments for encouraging children to uncover the relationships between science and technology—to begin to understand the relationships between natural laws and decisions made by humans that contravene or take advantage of those laws. What are the risks and tradeoffs of living in a brick and mortar apartment structure in California? What should building codes include? If you didn't have access to such technologies as weather satellites and radio communications, would you live in an isolated coastal area subject to hurricanes? Can you design a ship capable of carrying oil safely, even if a hole is punched in the hull? What recent technologies make shipping oil safer today than it was 30 to 40 years ago? Does use of an oil dispersant, a new technology, enhance or exacerbate an oil spill? Asking, and then struggling with answers to questions like these can help science and technology come alive in the classroom.

Most teachers who feel unprepared to teach science feel even less prepared to teach about technology. It is therefore important to encourage teachers to learn along with their students. Instruction, the vehicle of technology education, raises the same questions for "technophobes" as it does for the "science shy." Few people know how a refrigerator works, and fewer still can help a 4th grader develop an explanation of how it works. We need to experiment as a profession, to venture onto unfamiliar ground as we search for ways to help students learn about, and appreciate the effects of, more complex systems.

It is also important to make science and technology education available to all students, and to become sensitive to the reality of students who have had little exposure to technology outside the classroom. For example, because of cultural gender bias, girls may not have had as much opportunity to use computers as boys. Similarly, poor children, many of whom are minorities, may not have grown up surrounded by such household technologies as microwave ovens and VCRs. We need to provide classroom time to equalize their exposure to technology and technological issues.

Additionally, we must encourage the adoption of more technologically oriented, hands-on science activities. All too often, laboratory activities such as using magnets confirm basic science information but fail to model alternative approaches to solving problems, like the mechanics of using electromagnetic devices in cars and washing machines. Making technology tasks more open-ended and relevant to students' daily lives is the premise behind innovative programs such as Invent America! and science olympiads. These programs engage students in brainstorming solutions to difficult problems; students do, indeed, rise to the occasion and offer creative insights into these challenges.

LOCAL ROLES

Things to do now:

1. **Examine the current science curriculum** to determine how extensively topics and activities address technology or S/T/S-oriented issues. Is the treatment sufficient and appropriate? Decide on a plan of action that will modify the curriculum in keeping with the rationale and recommendations presented in this chapter. Work for administrative and school board approval for expanding the focus of the science curriculum to include the role of technology and S/T/S activities.

2. **Locate and examine technology and S/T/S-oriented materials and activities** (e.g., *Invent America!*, *Unified Science*, and *Mathematics for the Elementary School*). Create activities such as having children build models that do things. Discuss among colleagues which of the activities and materials can be integrated into your core science program. Invite parents and members of your community to contribute to this process.

3. **Collaborate with specialists in the social sciences** from local universities and your own school district and with career education specialists. As a team, develop ways to integrate technology and S/T/S issues into your core science curriculum.

Things to do for the future:

1. **Develop ongoing inservice programs** with and for teachers that give specific ideas and overall strategies for moving toward a more balanced science and technology program.

STATE ROLES

Things to do now:

1. **Call together** elementary teachers; specialists in science and technology education, the social sciences, and career education; and other curriculum leaders to examine your existing science curriculum guide or framework. Work to develop a new one that integrates technology and S/T/S issues. If such guides or frameworks are not appropriate in your state, have the group map a set of recommendations that local districts can consider as they develop their own science and technology curriculums.

2. **Establish a clearinghouse** to support the integration of technology into the science curriculum. The clearinghouse would focus on several tasks, including:

- Locating, purchasing, and cataloging appropriate curriculum materials that deal effectively with technology and S/T/S issues. Such items could be placed into a database that schools could access for review and possible adoption.
- Soliciting examples of schools and school districts that are models for the integration of science and technology. Make these examples known through the clearinghouse database.
- Working with business and industry councils to establish a database of technology examples that are appropriate for inclusion in an elementary science education program.
- Establishing a list of human resources—professionals from business and industry, higher education, and school districts—to assist local schools in integrating technology into the science curriculum.

Things to do for the future:

1. **Provide leadership in the development of assessment instruments and procedures** that adequately assess an integrated

science and technology approach as developed and implemented by schools. Such assessment should address program development as well as individual teacher use for improving instruction. Assessments must reflect an integrated program approach that actively involves children in creating and inventing as well as problem solving and decision making. An example of an appropriate assessment activity is asking the question, "what would humans need to live on Mars?"

2. **Coordinate the development of a statewide support system** of teachers, teacher educators, and staff developers. Such a network would provide preservice and inservice education that encourage the development of teachers who know how to effectively integrate science and technology and how to assess the newly developed programs.

MODELS AND RESOURCES

A Book: Mortimer Adler's (1982) *The Paideia Proposal: An Educational Manifesto* makes a case for a revitalized American education to include a structure and experiences that encourage students to examine academic and practical science, yielding a literacy that would include reading, writing, listening, calculating, observing, problem solving, and critical judgment.

State Models: A number of states—Florida, Indiana, Michigan, and New York, for example—have initiated efforts to strengthen the technology component of the science curriculum. Their policy statements and guides can provide models for others to consider.

An Organization: The Science through Science, Technology, and Society (S-STS) group at the Pennsylvania State University was formed to spearhead efforts at integrating technology into the curriculum. Funded in part by the National Science Foundation, it has produced several resources that can be vital for states and schools that wish to move in the science-technology direction, including:

• The *S-STS Reporter*, a quarterly newsletter that provides readers with up-to-date accounts of the S/T/S movement across the country, a review of curriculum materials in the S/T/S field, and timely articles on the S/T/S movement.

• An annual Technological Literacy Conference in Washington, D.C., each February, which brings together teachers, science and technology educators, and other professionals to present and share views on science through science, technology, and society.

• The National Association for Science, Technology, and Society (NASTS). This is an umbrella organization of scientists and engineers, K-12 educators, college and university educators, public interest groups, religion professionals, science policy personnel, and writers. The *S-STS Reporter* is available through NASTS by subscription alone or as part of membership in the organization.

Newsletters: A number of associations publish newsletters that can provide educators with guidance in developing the approach suggested in this chapter. They include the Pittsburgh Regional Center for Science Teachers; the Teachers' Clearinghouse for Science, Technology and Society; and the Humanities and Technology Association Newsletter.

Model District Curriculums: The Pittsburgh, Pennsylvania, school district and the Mt. Diablo Unified School District in Concord, California, produce materials that can be helpful to schools seeking model curriculum. The Jefferson County, Colorado, school district's publication, *The Primary Integrated Curriculum for First and Second Grades*, represents another model approach.

Curriculums from Other Countries:

• Under the direction of the Metropolitan Toronto School Board (1989), six Toronto area boards of education developed a guide for presenting technology in the elementary curriculum: *The Child's World: Presenting Technology to Children in the Primary and Junior Divisions*.

• Great Britain has a national curriculum that establishes three core subjects—English, mathematics, and science—and seven foundation subjects, including technology and design. This national effort also includes study programs and a major change in assessment practices.

Key References

Adler, M.J. (1982). *The Paideia Proposal: An Educational Manifesto*. New York: Macmillan.

American Association for the Advancement of Science. (1989). *Science for All Americans*. Washington, D.C.: AAAS.

Bybee, R. W., C. E. Buchwald, L. S. Crissman, D. Heil, P. J. Kuerbis, C. Matsumoto, and J. D. McInterney. (1989). *Science and Technology Education for the Elementary Years: Frameworks for Curriculum and*

Education for the Elementary Years: Frameworks for Curriculum and Instruction. Andover, Mass.: National Center for Improving Science Education, The NETWORK, Inc.

Department of Education and Science and the Welsh Office. (1989). *Science in the National Curriculum*. London: Her Majesty's Stationery Office.

Exxon Foundation. (1983). *Science Education in the United States: Essential Steps for Achieving Fundamental Improvement*. N.Y.: Exxon Foundation.

Hurd, P. D. (January 1986). "Perspectives for the Reform of Science Education." *Phi Delta Kappan* 67: 353-358.

Metropolitan Toronto School Board. (1989). *The Child's World: Presenting Technology to Children in the Primary and Junior Divisions*. Willowdale, Ontario, Canada: Metropolitan Toronto School Board.

National Science Board, Commission on Precollege Education for Mathematics, Science and Technology. (1983). *Educating Americans for the 21st Century*. Washington, D.C.: National Science Foundation.

National Science Teachers Association. (1982). *Science-Technology-Society: Science Education for the 1980s*. Washington, D.C.: NSTA.

4.
Include Scientific Attitudes and Skills as Important Goals

Science education can make an important contribution to student learning beyond basic scientific knowledge through developing positive attitudes and valuable skills. Scientific attitudes, positive attitudes toward science and one's self, and both laboratory and intellectual skills are all part of the attitude/skill package.

WHAT WE KNOW

Children come to elementary school excited about exploring the world around them. They constantly ask questions and search for answers. They wonder about the world they live in and what makes it work. If we don't take advantage of this curiosity and hunger for knowledge when they are young, little else we do will matter as they get older. Part of the job of the elementary science program is to build on this good, natural start with opportunities to explore and better understand the natural world through constructivist science programs. Such programs are the best vehicles for ensuring that scientific attitudes are nurtured and encouraged over time.

> Attitudes, some of which are unique to the study of science and technology, are inherent in scientific and technological enterprises. Indeed, where would we be if Einstein didn't have a thirst for knowledge or a respect for reason in his ventures? And where will we be if people who are *not* scientists don't want to know how science and technology can contribute to solving world problems like hunger, pollution, and the threat of war.

Scientific attitudes, however, are rarely developed in elementary students (or in most people, for that matter). For instance, at an early age many kids believe that words in print represent the truth. The scientific attitude of skepticism is therefore important to foster. Children also tend to think that everything has a right and wrong answer. While there are certainly some right answers, more often than not, ambiguity is something all scientists must learn to accept. How, then, can we promote the development of scientific attitudes? If we provide children with opportunities to do and learn science and technology, a separate lesson on the need for accepting ambiguity would be unnecessary. With the right experiences, scientific attitudes will evolve.

What are some important scientific attitudes or "habits of mind"? They include:

• *Desiring knowledge*: viewing science as a way of knowing and understanding.

• *Being skeptical*: recognizing the appropriate time and place to question authoritarian statements and "self-evident truths."

• *Relying on data*: explaining natural occurrences by collecting and ordering information, testing ideas, and respecting the facts that are revealed.

• *Accepting ambiguity*: recognizing that data are rarely clear and compelling, and appreciating the new questions and problems that arise.

• *Willingness to modify explanations*: seeing new possibilities in the data.

• *Cooperating in answering questions and solving problems*: working together to pool ideas, explanations, and solutions.

• *Respecting reason*: valuing patterns of thought that lead from data to conclusions and, eventually, to the construction of theories.

• *Being honest*: viewing information objectively, without bias.

Elementary school children also need to develop positive attitudes toward science and toward themselves. Good elementary science programs strive to help children maintain or develop a sense of awe, curiosity, creativity, and the use of scientific resources to develop explanations about the natural world. Figuring out what it takes for plants to grow, lighting a light bulb and determining why it works one way and not another—these successes, so unlike many outcomes of schoolwork, should make children feel good about gaining more control over their world.

In addition to positive attitudes, **a good science program can help develop different kinds of skills.** First, children can develop *laboratory skills*, such as the ability to read a thermometer, use a balance, and focus a microscope. Second, they can develop the set of *intellectual skills* needed to apply the methods of science, such as the ability to generate a hypothesis; design an experiment to test the hypothesis; and collect, process, and interpret data. Third, children can develop *generic thinking skills*, such as problem solving and reasoning. Finally, science experiences can help children develop reading, mathematics, and oral and written *communications skills*.

Good science activities begin with a question or a problem, and skills are developed and applied by pursuing answers and solutions. One way of organizing the necessary skills uses three levels:

1. **Information gathering** (including research): an initial step in answering scientific questions or solving technological problems. Some information-gathering skills are communicating, measuring, and questioning.

2. **Problem solving:** the *process* of answering scientific questions and solving technological problems. Skills include the ability to state questions, identify problems, develop hypotheses, predict, infer, design experiments, and interpret data. New skills that are technologically important include the ability to identify alternative solutions and to assess their costs, risks, and benefits.

3. **Decision making:** although not typically considered a science skill, it warrants attention because it's an obvious extension of skills typically incorporated in science programs. Critical and analytical thinking skills, for example, are in many ways the basis for making decisions. Further, decision making is needed for solving technological problems.

TAKING ACTION ON WHAT WE KNOW

The very nature of constructivist science learning should foster the development of scientific skills and positive attitudes. Let's go back to Ms. Lopez's 2nd grade class to get an idea of what good skill and attitude development can look like.

Ms. Lopez's science curriculum is built on topics of high interest to her 2nd graders, with development of the ten major concepts worked appropriately into her activities. But fostering basic science knowledge is only part of Ms. Lopez's plan for science education. She knows that constructing knowledge from firsthand experience while using the skills that scientists use in the process of doing science helps students to develop valuable skills and dispositions toward using science. Ms. Lopez relies not only on the children's natural curiosity, but also on cooperative groups where the work and the responsibility for getting tasks done are shared. Success, pride, and a sense of accomplishment are experienced by all.

In her class's study of seeds, Ms. Lopez pursues these skill and attitude goals as she teaches major concepts such as diversity, cycles, and structure and function. She began the seeds unit by acknowledging that students needed to unbundle their previous conceptions about seeds to begin to construct their own meaning for the major concepts. After several weeks of exciting exploration, her 2nd graders had indeed accomplished this. And it was the process of exploration and discovery in studying seeds that helped to maintain their interest in science learning and their abilities to untangle the mystery of their initial questions about seeds. In addition, Ms. Lopez's inquiry style of learning opened the door for further questions and ideas about how other things grow, what other life cycles look like, and where else one can find diversity—all of which led to a quest for more science learning.

Knowing that they were truly behaving as scientists also encouraged the students to develop scientific attitudes and skills. Ms. Lopez continually reinforced this throughout the lessons by sharing with them the fact that scientists do exactly what the children did in class: ask questions, look for answers by exploring the question as a problem to solve, observe and measure findings carefully, communicate ideas clearly in both written and illustrative modes, keep accurate records of data, know that it is acceptable and helpful to challenge ideas, test and retest ideas, work with others to find answers, and be willing to modify original ideas. In addition, these tasks challenged the students to develop both communication and manipulative skills.

It is not enough to assume that science education automatically promotes the development of positive attitudes and valuable skills, even if the program is a good one. Teachers, administrators, and policy makers must plan for ways that learning science can incorporate attention to the skills and attitudes we value.

LOCAL ROLES

Things to do now:

1. Review current curriculum goals and materials to check that they reflect the importance of teaching attitudes and skills. Where they don't, incorporate materials and strategies for fostering positive attitudes and valuable skills. Curriculum guides need to articulate how to integrate skill development with the development of major scientific concepts. Give special attention to how hands-on activities and the discussion of science and technology issues can use and foster the skills of information gathering, decision making, and problem solving along with scientific habits of mind.

2. Be sure that programs that recognize excellent science and technology education practices in schools and classrooms also pay attention to the development of skills and attitudes. Teachers or school programs that do a good job of developing these attitudes and skills should be identified and used as models for others to try.

3. Assess how well the development of attitudes and skills is incorporated into daily instruction. (See Chapter 10 for specific strategies.) Use informal assessments such as skill and attitude checklists to record student growth over time.

Things to do for the future:

1. Prepare teachers at both the preservice and inservice level to advance the development of skills and attitudes by (1) helping them know what the skills and attitudes of science are, and (2) showing them how constructivist science programs, instructional methods, and assessment strategies can be used to reinforce the development of positive attitudes and valuable skills.

2. Educate the community about the importance of skills and attitudes, as well as knowledge goals, for elementary science education.

STATE ROLES

Things to do now:

1. Include the goals of scientific skill and attitude development in state curriculum guides.

2. Advise, monitor, and lend guidance to preservice and inservice programs to encourage curriculum and instruction that include the development of valuable skills and positive attitudes. Work with state and professional organizations to provide inservice programs that emphasize these competencies.

3. Collaborate with universities, informal science education centers, and other science resource centers to identify, develop, maintain, and disseminate materials and programs that promote skills and attitudes in classroom materials and for teacher development. Promote constructivist science programs as a powerful learning tool for generating positive attitudes and skill development.

Things to do for the future:

Work with districts to produce state guidelines for incorporating skill and attitude development as part of the overall goals of science education. Develop an agreed-upon set of terms to describe desired results in these areas, and make sure that state credentialing boards require methods courses consistent with the sanctioned guidelines for incorporating skills and attitudes. Then inform district administrators about the new guidelines and ask for their support by having them promote the guidelines at the district level.

MODELS AND RESOURCES

A State Model: The New York Elementary Science Syllabus includes a model for problem solving in its goals for elementary school science instruction.

A State Model: The California Science Framework includes as goals for students science processes that are used by scientists, including observing, communicating, comparing, inferring, and applying. It encourages teachers to engage students in activities where they have responsibility for tasks that call for development and use of these processes. Further, the framework encourages teachers to help children consider the values and ethics related to the effects of science on society.

A Model Curriculum: Improving Urban Elementary Science, a science curriculum currently under development by the Education Development Center (EDC) and Sunburst, includes a balance of attitudes, skills, knowledge, and values in its science content.

A Model Curriculum: The Kids Network, under development by the Technical Education Research Centers (TERC) in collaboration with the National Geographic Society, is a telecommunications-based science curriculum for grades 4-6. It intends specifically to improve student attitudes toward science, giving children skills that allow them access to science and that foster scientific literacy. In Kid's Network activities, children are encouraged to ask meaningful questions, collect accurate data, organize information, and use observations and data to answer questions.

Key References

American Association for the Advancement of Science. (1989). *Science for All Americans.* Washington, D.C.: AAAS.

Bybee, R. W. (1986). "The Sisyphean Question in Science Education: What Should the Scientifically and Technologically Literate Person Know, Value, and Do?" In *Science-Technology-Society*, 1985 Yearbook of the National Science Teachers Association. Washington, D.C.: NSTA.

Bybee, R. W., C. E. Buchwald, L. S. Crissman, D. Heil, P. J. Kuerbis, C. Matsumoto, and J. D. McInerney. (1989). *Science and Technology Education for the Elementary Years: Frameworks for Curriculum and Instruction.* Andover, Mass.: The National Center for Improving Science Education, The NETWORK, Inc.

National Science Board Commission on Precollege Education in Mathematics, Science and Technology. (1983). *Educating Americans for the 21st Century.* Washington, D.C.: NSB.

Padilla, M. (1986). "The Science Process Skills." *Research Matters . . . to the Science Teacher*, newsletter of the National Association for Research on Science Teaching, 3.

5.
View Science Learning from a Constructivist Perspective

During constructivist learning, students have the opportunity to verbalize, test, modify, and even abandon their pre-existing ideas and adopt new ones. Through learning tasks keyed to their developmental levels, students have the chance to make sense of the world by actively constructing meaning out of natural phenomena and their everyday experiences.

WHAT WE KNOW

There are several good reasons for taking a thoughtful look at the constructivist view of learning. First, we know that **what is already in the learner's mind matters. The constructivist paradigm builds on this important understanding by paying attention to the prior knowledge that students bring to each learning experience.** A teacher who assesses what students already know by asking questions about friction, for example, may find that one child understands it as "something," a force that slows down the motion of another object—like a bicycle in sand. Further inquiry may demonstrate that the child falsely believes that there is no friction when she slides down a schoolyard slide because of the fast speed. By using a constructivist orientation, teachers give students the opportunity to verbalize their understanding of a given concept and then build on that framework to help kids consider and test new ideas about the concept. Students can construct a much truer understanding of the concept of friction, for example, through tasks that match their cognitive abilities; elementary age students can do so by exploring objects in contact with one another, the generation of heat, and the varying degrees of friction.

We also know that **exemplary science learning is promoted by both hands-on and minds-on instructional techniques—the foundations of constructivist learning.** Hands-on activities are critical for science learning, particularly because elementary students are at the concrete stage of their cognitive development. But often teachers don't use these activities to help students think deeply about what they observe and experience. The minds-on half of the constructivist equation is missing. There is a need to do more than just science activities to promote higher order thinking and student understanding of major scientific concepts. For instance, students who are challenged to make a piece of clay float in water will learn much from their trials about weight, sinking and floating, surface tension, and density—all of which will enhance their growing understanding of several major organizing concepts, such as cause and effect, scale, and models. Students will develop their thinking skills and assimilate new ideas into their conceptual frameworks as they experiment with factors like the boat's surface area, the amount of water displaced, and the amount of cargo a boat can carry, and by asking questions of themselves, their peers, and the resources (including the teacher) they count on in the process of constructing new understandings.

Compare this example of constructivist learning with the task sometimes used in science classes of following directions for making a boat that floats. Hands-on activities alone can amount to little more than busy work. We need to ask whether or not instruction furthers students' conceptual understanding of how things work. When science is taught and learned as a recipe, learners fail to make meaning of the new ideas. Constructivist learning happens when students develop new understandings as a result of making sense of their own experiences. Indeed, individuals learn by actively experiencing the physical environment and through social interaction. In this way they construct their own knowledge. **Constructivism includes the important hands-on part of science instruction, but enriches learning by promoting concept development and higher order thinking skills through ample opportunities to engage in dialogue with the teacher and peers.** Thus, constructivism is markedly different from teacher-dominated and -directed instruction, as well as an important refinement of the hands-on, discovery-oriented instruction that has been prevalent in some science classrooms. As Hawkins (1983) has stated:

> A part—indeed a major part—of the structuring of our minds must come from instruction. But this obvious statement leads much too easily to notions that are, I believe, radically false. *In*struction by a teacher fails without a matching construction by the learner. . . (p. 73)

Children bring their own ideas to science lessons. For instance, contrast the scientist's perspective of plants to a child's view.

Scientist's Perspective: A plant is a producer.

Child's View: A plant is something that grows in a garden. Carrots and cabbage from the garden are not plants; they are vegetables. Trees are not plants; they are plants when they are little, but when they grow up they are not plants. Seeds are not plants. Dandelions are not plants; they are weeds. Plants . . . have multiple sources of food. Photosynthesis is not important to plants (Osborne and Freyberg 1985).

How do teachers help children move their thinking so that it is more aligned with the scientifically accepted view? In Ms. Lopez's class (see Introduction, pp. xv-xvii), recall that the children took several weeks to actively explore their ideas about seeds. They started by listing what they knew about seeds, and from this information Ms. Lopez made decisions about future activities for the class. Using a combination of instructional techniques—individual, small group, and large group—Ms. Lopez encouraged the children to share their perceptions, conduct experiments, question each other's understandings, and gradually incorporate new ideas. Throughout the unit of study, Ms. Lopez encouraged the children to carefully reconstruct their knowledge of seeds and plants—to make meaning of old knowledge and new information from various sources, including experiments and dialogues with each other—and to gain more refined views of such major concepts as diversity, life cycles, and structure and function

If students are not given the opportunity to express their ideas, then they are only passively, if at all, confronting the explanations of accepted science. Neither the students nor the teacher is aware of a conflict if one exists. Passive science teaching techniques simply "pour in" more information on top of pre-existing ideas. The students, in trying to assimilate the new information, will assess whether or not it "fits." If it doesn't, students will hold onto the notion already in place, thinking, "It's worked fine so far," thereby rejecting the new, scientifically correct information. Often they will retain the new information only as long as needed to regurgitate it on tests.

Learning often involves conceptual change. When children have the opportunity to test their ideas, they may not only add to or extend their existing concepts, but may end up radically re-organizing their conceptual framework. For example, a child might know that you can grow fruits and vegetables from seeds and may also understand that there are seeds inside fruits and vegetables. In testing this notion, students might be surprised to find no seeds upon cutting open a carrot! A knowledgeable teacher will then provide ways for the student to investigate and propose possible explanations why the carrot—a root—has no seeds and where the seeds of the carrot plant might be found. Here, the *method* by which the concepts of change, structure, and function are introduced helps children to reorganize existing beliefs.

Constructivism asks us to rethink our assumptions about learning and, consequently, about instruction. Learning is not passive. On the contrary, the very nature of constructing meaning is that the students make links between prior knowledge and newly generated ideas and do so in a process that involves continual checking and restructuring. No longer can we conceive of instruction as something teachers do to or for students. Individuals as learners set their own goals and control their own learnings. The final responsibility for learning rests not with the teacher, but with the learner.

Finally, **the end product of constructivist learning is much more than rote memorization.** Instead, it's understanding how processes work, and why that information is useful. This leads the children to ask, wonder, and answer, and then to ask again in a way that is meaningful to them. It is the same type of understanding that eventually leads the scientist to describe and explain a new set of phenomena and the engineer to develop a new and useful application.

The constructivist view of learning clearly has implications for teaching strategies and the roles of both teacher and student. The teacher becomes a diagnostician, a prescriber of appropriate learning activities, and a facilitator of learning. The role of students in this model shifts from "passive sponge" to "active player," where they are responsible for their own learning by developing their own theories, comparing their theories with those of other classmates, and summarizing and displaying their theories (Scott et al. 1987).

The constructivist view of learning is not a neat little package that offers a pat formula for teaching science. It does, however, call for an instructional model that is based on this view of how students learn. Such a model is described in Chapter 6. The remaining recommendations in this book regarding teaching, assessment, and teacher development are all based on a constructivist perspective.

TAKING ACTION ON WHAT WE KNOW

Few educators are currently using an instructional approach that accommodates the constructivist perspective. On the contrary, constructivism is only now emerging from cognitive research as a concept, and it baffles, scares, and even annoys a large portion of educators. Taking time to elicit students' preconceived notions and engaging students in in-depth exploratory activities are new behaviors for many teachers who learned science and how to teach it in conventional ways. It's therefore important to prepare teachers so that they feel comfortable and supported in doing the type of instruction that echoes a constructivist approach. For examples of what this would look like, see Figure 5.1.

How can we help teachers adopt a constructivist view so that it plays a viable role in their instructional practices? Start by spelling out the benefits of constructivism in an appealing, nonthreatening way to all educators, and to elementary teachers in particular. Then work toward narrowing the gap between the constructivist view and the science goals we hold for students by familiarizing teachers with this learning process. **Make it clear that the constructivist perspective permeates all new curriculum approaches, not just those for science.** This is especially true

---

Figure 5.1
Are You Using a Constructivist Approach?

You're well into constructivist teaching if you:

- Encourage and accept student autonomy, initiation, and leadership.
- Allow student thinking to drive lessons. Shift content and instructional strategy based on student responses.
- Ask students to elaborate on their responses.
- Allow wait time after asking questions.
- Encourage students to interact with each other and with you.
- Ask thoughtful, open-ended questions.
- Encourage students to reflect on experiences and predict future outcomes.
- Ask students to articulate their theories about concepts before presenting your understanding of the concepts.
- Look for students' alternative conceptions and design lessons to address any misconceptions.

(Source: Brooks 1990)

---

for "whole language" curriculums, which stress beginning with children's own experiences, active learning, and constructing one's own meaning. Helping elementary teachers see connections across disciplines will prevent them from viewing each curriculum area as separate, requiring them to once again do different things.

Teachers need to know about children's early views of natural phenomena. Once aware of children's common (mis)conceptions related to such concepts as those described in Chapter 2, teachers will begin to understand and recognize children's alternative frameworks. Efforts to map children's conceptions of science concepts are cited in the Key References section of this chapter.

One of the most effective strategies for fostering constructivist learning is to **use an instructional model that advances conceptual change** (see Chapter 6). Such an instructional framework would then need to be used with instructional materials and strategies that reflect the constructivist view of learning, both within the science program and across the curriculum.

A wide variety of instructional materials lend themselves to constructivist teaching, including some veteran programs from the 1960s. How is a constructivist approach similar to, and dissimilar from, the earlier hands-on programs? Let's examine one such program, the Science Curriculum Improvement Study (SCIS), to see. At first glance, there are great similarities between SCIS and the constructivist learning and teaching model. First, there is a curriculum parallel: Both focus on teaching for depth rather than breadth, for instance, by stressing major concepts. Second, there is an instructional similarity: Both use a learning-teaching cycle that begins with children engaging in concrete activities before exploring a concept abstractly. In both, there is then opportunity for children to apply their new knowledge in different contexts, cementing their new conceptual frameworks.

For many SCIS teachers, especially those who use the SCIS program as a framework rather than a curriculum that is followed step-by-step, the differences between the SCIS approach and constructivism are subtle rather than striking. What are some differences? First, the teacher has to play the role of diagnostician, assessing children's prior knowledge and making judgments about activities—including some that may not be in the SCIS curriculum—that can help children think anew about a concept. Second, the teacher does not introduce the concept; rather, he introduces new information and poses challenging questions, facilitating the children's active construction of a concept. This may take considerable time—longer than what many SCIS teachers typically allow—because when children are forced to move ahead faster than they can accommodate new information, they resort to memorizing the information and forcing it into their conceptual frameworks, which are left unchanged. Finally, the developers of the SCIS program chose to build units of study directly on the major concepts they believed were important. While we believe science programs should be conceptually rich, organizing around major concepts is only one method. Being sensitive to "the child's curriculum" is another. There are many topics or themes—seeds, for example—that can be taught to children with opportunities to give up old ideas and develop new understandings, while studying topics that are inherently interesting to them.

As the results of cognitive research become more known and accepted, more curriculums and materials are apt to use a constructive approach to science education. For example, as noted in the Models and Resources section of this chapter, some newly developed, NSF-funded projects have a constructivist perspective consciously imbedded into their materials.

State science specialists need to **promote the usefulness of the constructivist approach so that its meaning and techniques penetrate the collective consciousness of educators and the public.** As a first step, formulate and identify the terminology and intention of this meaning-centered approach in terms of curriculum. While we don't want to create the buzzwords and holy grail of fads in instructional methods, it is necessary to produce a lexicon that educators and others can use to share and refine their craft. This means more extensive presentations, publishing, and policymaking that focus on how classrooms will benefit from a constructivist approach.

Next, **look at state and local guidelines for elementary science curriculum and instruction, and make sure that they advocate a constructivist view of learning.** To be effective, this effort must provide concrete, visual examples of how instruction will differ from (and improve) current practice to help classroom teachers develop the understanding and skills to make meaning-centered science a reality at the elementary school level.

Inservice programs for classroom teachers as well as administrators will need to be established to help schools adopt the constructivist approach. The character of such training ought to accentuate the performance-oriented skills elementary teachers already possess, like arts education. Some elementary teachers and their principals may already be familiar with the essential meaning of constructivist learning through hands-on, inquiry-based programs, though they may not be familiar with the term "constructivism." Inservice programs need to model the essence of this approach by having teachers use their prior experiences and ideas about scientific phenomena in learning new ways to teach science.

LOCAL ROLES

Things to do now:

1. **Promote the benefits of employing a constructivist perspective** across the curriculum, and for science instruction in particular, to teachers and administrators.

2. **Establish a teacher support group** whose members are interested in constructivism. Read and discuss articles, share resources and classroom experiences, and so on.

Things to do for the future:

1. **Develop inservice programs** for teachers in which they learn to facilitate students' constructing meaning in a variety of situations.

2. **Videotape lessons of teachers** who use constructivist methods, and use them as learning and promotional tools in professional development projects for teachers, administrators, and the community at large.

3. **Work with administrators and school board members** so that they observe early trials with these techniques to witness how well they work and how different they look from current practice.

4. **Acquire or develop instructional materials** that align with science and technology goals and promote constructivist learning.

STATE ROLES

Things to do now:

Identify instructional materials, including software, that stimulate learning by meaning and through experiences, rather than by rote. Develop a list and distribute it through appropriate channels. Provide opportunities for school people to see and experiment with sample materials.

Things to do for the future:

1. **Collaborate with state professional associations** to begin to develop a cadre of specialists and lead teachers who can advocate and start constructivist-oriented staff development efforts in regions throughout the state.

2. **Identify exemplary teachers, schools, and districts** as models to demonstrate for others in the state the effectiveness and benefits of putting constructivist teaching into practice.

3. **Work with universities to offer preservice programs** that feature constructivist learning theory and techniques.

MODELS AND RESOURCES

The following models and resources will prove useful for schools and teachers making an effort to further constructivist-inspired instruction.

A Book: In *Children's Ideas in Science*, Rosalind Driver and her associates (1985) cover children's ideas about a wide range of natural phenomena, illustrating how ideas change and develop via teaching. Although it focuses on middle and secondary science education, elementary teachers will find the book's insights helpful.

A Local Model: Shoreham-Wading River School District in Long Island, New York, is a suburban-rural district of about 2,000 students that integrates a constructivist orientation across the curriculum. The district prepares teachers to ask questions rather than disseminate information, pose contradictions rather than point out mistakes, search for student hypotheses instead of explain standard theories, and press students to use past knowledge rather than assume they come to class with blank slates. Students often work in small groups to solve self-generated problems, make journal entries, and design and conduct research. At the elementary level, the district employs a science resource teacher who offers assistance with organizing resources, planning, and instruction.

Model Curriculums: The National Science Foundation (NSF) has funded eight major (and several other) elementary materials development programs that lean toward constructivist instruction (see Chapter 6). Many of the elementary curriculums sponsored by the NSF in the mid-sixties also had a constructivist bent. The new CD-ROM Science Helper, assembled by Mary Budd Rowe, compiles excellent lessons from these materials that contribute to constructivist learning.

An Association: The Association for Constructivist Teaching in Worthington, Massachusetts, identifies and disseminates effective constructivist practices in both the professional cultures of teachers and the learning environments of children. Members receive a quarterly newsletter, *The Constructivist*, and have an annual conference.

An International Project: The Children's Learning in Science Project, based at the University of Leeds, England, probes student understanding of scientific concepts and develops, implements, and evaluates teaching strategies that promote better conceptual understanding in science.

Key References

Brooks, J. G. (February 1990). "Teachers and Students: Constructivists Forging New Connections." *Educational Leadership* 47, 5: 68-71.

Driver, R., E. Guesne, and A. Tiberghien. (1985). *Children's Ideas in Science.* Philadelphia: Open University Press.

Duckworth, E. (1987). *The Having of Wonderful Ideas and Other Essays on Teaching and Learning.* New York: Teachers College Press.

Hawkins, D. (Spring 1983). "Nature Closely Observed." *Daedalus* 112: 65-90.

Marek, E. A. (December 1986). "They Misunderstand But They'll Pass." *The Science Teacher* 53: 32-35.

Osborne R., and P. Freyberg. (1985). *Learning in Science: The Implications of Children's Science.* Portsmouth, N.H.: Heinemann.

Proceedings of the Second International Seminar: Misconceptions and Educational Strategies In Science and Mathematics. (July 1987). Ithaca, N.Y.: Cornell University.

Scott, P., T. Dyson, and S. Gater. (1987). *A Constructivist View of Learning and Teaching in Science.* Leeds, England: Children's Learning in Science Project, Centre for Studies in Science and Mathematics Education, The University of Leeds.

Stephans, J. I., et al. (September 1986). "Misconceptions Die Hard." *The Science Teacher* 53: 65-69.

Thier, H. D. (March 1986). *Heads On Elementary Science: The Challenge for the Nineties.* (Council for Elementary Science International Monograph and Occasional Paper Series #1.) Washington, D.C.: National Science Teachers Association.

6.
Use a Constructivist-Oriented Instructional Model to Guide Learning

Good instructional models promote the same mechanisms that scientists use when they "do science" by inviting children to take a more meaningful look at their world and then challenging them to make sense of and take action on what they are learning.

WHAT WE KNOW

We need to re-examine instructional frameworks that foster passive, individualistic, and competitive learning and that do not take into account the many different styles of student learning. We need to ask whether instruction that is characterized by lectures, teacher demonstrations, and text readings furthers the constructivist learning that we value for science education. Exemplary teaching models promote what we value by providing useful opportunities for learners to articulate, test, share, and act on their ideas and findings.

Sound instructional models promote the notion that science is what scientists do, as well as what they know. Beyond the grades students earn by memorizing new information, such models value how well students use their new knowledge and incorporate it into their old views.

Noteworthy instructional models for science and technology learning need to be consistent with the way scientific and technological investigations are typically carried out. No one enjoys or learns from being told how things are; most people learn by finding out for themselves. Solid instructional models have students doing science and technology by engaging them in the acts of exploratory investigations, constructing meaning out of their findings, proposing tentative explanations and solutions, exploring concepts again, and then evaluating concepts in reference to their own lives. Our model (Figure 6.1) reflects these characteristics in a four-stage format in which students:

- Accept an invitation to learn;
- Explore, discover, and create;
- Propose explanations and solutions; and
- Take action on what they learned.

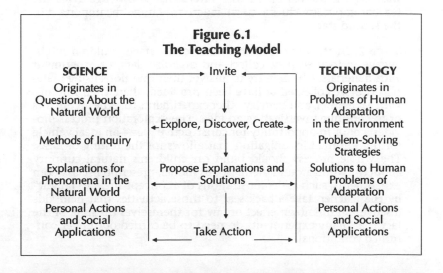

Figure 6.1
The Teaching Model

SCIENCE		TECHNOLOGY
	Invite	
Originates in Questions About the Natural World		Originates in Problems of Human Adaptation in the Environment
Methods of Inquiry	Explore, Discover, Create	Problem-Solving Strategies
Explanations for Phenomena in the Natural World	Propose Explanations and Solutions	Solutions to Human Problems of Adaptation
Personal Actions and Social Applications	Take Action	Personal Actions and Social Applications

Although the four stages are presented sequentially, the practicing scientist or engineer rarely, if ever, follows the model step by step. The figure, with its arrows and loops, illustrates the complex nature of scientific investigations and technological problem solving. In the classroom, after initial engagement, the children and teacher may perform exploratory investigations, propose and invent tentative explanations or solutions, and explore concepts several times before coming to the last step: taking action on what they have learned. Even then, the explorations and refinements continue.

Imagine the excitement of the research scientist who finds himself or herself fully engaged in the investigative process. We can promote that same exhilaration in kids with science learning that employs the type of model proposed here.

Stage 1. The process begins by engaging the learner with an *invitation to learn*. It may be sparked by a child's spontaneous question or by a teacher-generated question about the natural world (science) or a problem in human adaptation (technology) that's elicited by events such as the Exxon Valdez oil spill or the Armenian earthquake. Such events stimulate immediate questions that students and teacher may ponder together. It includes the recognition of prior conceptions and beliefs held by children by giving them time to communicate through discussion, illustrations, and writing about their impressions and understandings of the question or problem at hand. In the case of an oil spill, for example, teachers might find that students believe that animals and birds affected by the spill can take care of the oil on their fur and feathers simply by washing themselves off in the water. This knowledge gives the teacher important clues as to what activities might be important in the second stage.

Stage 2. In the *explore, discover, and create* stage, children might engage in focused play, collect and organize data, or experiment with materials. Children try to answer their questions using materials they've collected or have been provided, share their findings with each other, and then try other experiments to settle arguments or to continue investigating an idea. The exploration process provides a built-in opportunity for constructive play—an ideal vehicle for the informal investigation that allows for the testing of ideas. The whole process should build on children's natural curiosity about the world around them. In this model, prescriptive classroom experiments, such as demonstrations of a concept already "taught" by the teacher, take a back seat to those activities that help kids discover an unknown effect or law for themselves (in spite of the fact that many experiments do need to be carried out under controlled conditions).

Let's nurture the precious place that discovery holds in the world of science by providing the types of learning experiences that honor it, while recognizing that the experiences are specifically planned to allow the children to hone in on particular concepts.

For example, children may try floating feathers from sea gulls on water and note what happens: the length of time the feathers float, what they look like when they are wet, how well they float, and how long it takes them to dry off. Students can then compare these findings with feathers soaked in diluted motor oil.

Stage 3. As learners *propose explanations and solutions* that are based on their own observations, they construct a new view of the concept under study. Students are therefore changing their prior conceptions based on the new information gained through exploration and discovery. They persuade themselves, as well as their peers, that the new conception is based on convincing data from activities about which they have firsthand knowledge.

In the case of oily feathers, students will undoubtedly form an opinion about bird feathers coated with oil and the inability of water to fully dissolve the oil. Here they may be drawn again into Stage 2 of the model as they try to answer questions about how to remove the oil from fur and feathers.

Stage 4. The process of constructing a fresh view prepares students to *take action on what they learned*, and doing so demonstrates that they have truly integrated the newly discovered information and proposed explanations into their existing conceptual frameworks. The teacher has not taught a particular concept but, rather, has provided appropriate activities, questioning, and the environment in which the children have constructed a new conceptual understanding. Regarding the oil spill, students may decide to take action by writing letters to officials of oil companies that contain recommended solutions (and their rationales) for future oil spills, or they might write Congress to express their opinions about related policies, noting how they arrived at their opinions (i.e., their conceptual understandings).

Figure 6.2 is a more detailed depiction of the instructional model, with teaching examples for both science and technology.

Figure 6.2
The Teaching Model

Teaching Examples for Science	Stages in the Teaching Model	Teaching Examples for Technology

Invitation

Observe the natural world	Observe the human-made world
Ask questions about the natural world	Recognize a human problem
State possible hypotheses	Identify possible solutions

Explorations, Discoveries, Creations

Engage in focused play	Brainstorm possible alternatives
Look for information	Experiment with materials
Observe specific phenomena	Design a model
Collect and organize data	Employ problem-solving strategies
Select appropriate resources	Discuss solutions with others
Design and conduct experiments	Evaluate choices
Engage in debate	Identify risks and consequences
Define parameters of an investigation	Analyze data

Proposing Explanations and Solutions

Communicate information and ideas	Construct and explain a model
Construct a new explanation	Constructively review a solution
Evaluation by peers	Express multiple answers/solutions
Determine appropriate closure	Integrate a solution with existing knowledge and experiences

Taking Action

Apply knowledge and skills	Make decisions
Share information and ideas	Transfer knowledge and skills
Ask new questions	Develop products and promote ideas

Note: Although this figure has two distinct columns, a review of teaching examples clearly shows that science and technology are intertwined; many of the examples could easily be placed in both columns. Communicating information and ideas, for example, is as much a part of science as it is a part of technology.

The instructional framework proposed herein serves as a guide for teachers to use while creating lesson plans and, at a macro level, unit plans. What does this instructional model look like in action? We have already seen one example, that of Ms. Lopez, who used the model to plan a flexible sequence of activities on seeds for her 2nd graders (see Introduction, pp. xv-xvii). Recall that she began by informally assessing her students' knowledge about seeds, planned a series of exploratory activities, and worked with the children to design experiments that produced information that they could incorporate into their developing science conceptual frameworks. While the children amassed a wealth of information about seeds through the carefully planned activities, Ms. Lopez kept them focused on major conceptual ideas, such as those mentioned in Chapter 2. It was the *major* ideas she sought to nurture in the children, knowing that they could use these ideas to make sense of a potential factual overload and, perhaps, also uncover links to such non-science areas as mathematics and social studies.

We get another view of the instructional model by visiting Mr. Clark, a 4th grade teacher and colleague of Ms. Lopez.

For a number of years, Mr. Clark has taught a popular unit on batteries and bulbs that his college methods instructor introduced to him. In most years, the unit was simply great fun for his students. Sometimes it lasted up to six or eight weeks, with a few students pursuing activities throughout the rest of the school year. In other years, the magic just wasn't there and the activities lasted only a few weeks. This was perplexing to Mr. Clark, but even more bothersome was his persistent hunch that while the kids generally had fun and learned a lot about electricity, he was unsure what the kids really understood. Did all of them have an accurate notion of electrical circuits, resistors, and the differences between parallel and series circuits? In spite of an eloquent defense to his colleagues (and in a few cases to parents and children!) over the importance of this unit and the need for children to engage in the processes of science, the picture did not seem complete.

This year was to be different, however. At meetings at the beginning of the school year, Ms. Lopez shared with her colleagues some information and activities she became acquainted with during a summer science education institute two years ago. She introduced Mr. Clark and the other teachers to the elements of constructivist learning and the four-step instructional model, and she gave them examples from the seeds unit she had designed and taught last spring. Mr. Clark saw a way to refine his batteries and bulbs unit. As he studied Figure 6.2, he saw how he could provide more structure to what sometimes turned into nothing but fun discovery activities. For example, he realized that after students had explored an idea through concrete activities, he could probe their thinking and have them post on classroom walls the diagrams of circuits that worked and those that didn't, so that they all could discuss what constituted a circuit. Even more important, he saw how he could get the children to focus on a major concept, like systems, through activities on the subconcept of circuits. To help with his planning, he set up a large chart on butcher paper, like that in Figure 6.3, and began to list possible activities in the two columns. Eventually, he developed several charts. One detailed the general flow of possible activities over the length of the unit. Others detailed a sequence for just one day. Some focused on only one stage—for example, exploration, since he believed that the children needed more time on this stage.

	Figure 6.3 A Framework for Planning	
Stage	What the children will do	What the teacher will do
Invitation		
Explore		
Explain		
Take action		

As he redesigned the unit from what he had done in previous years, Mr. Clark knew a good starting point would be for students to struggle with understanding what defined a circuit. Later he would tie this understanding to the concept of a system. In the initial lesson, besides creating an operational definition of a circuit, he wanted to watch students engage in the processes of observation, inference, and communication. He knew some students would become frustrated with their initial efforts, so he made a conscious attempt to promote the attitudes of persistence, desiring knowledge, and cooperation in discovering and sharing information. On the first day of the unit, each child was presented with one battery, one bulb, and one wire. The invitation to learn was, "How can you make this bulb light?"

In teams of three, the children worked to discover a solution to the problem (question). One child in each team was charged with keeping a record of all of the team's creations and inventions, regardless of whether or not they worked. Another child was designated as a reporter and posted the team's findings on newsprint with a large-scale drawing of each attempt. The cooperative learning skills that Mr. Clark had taught the students earlier in the year really paid off. The drawings were referred to time and time again when the students looked for new ideas to solve the problem of how to make the bulb light. The drawings also served as a means of communication to explain their trials. Mr. Clark pointed out that scientists keep track of their successes and failures because they learn from both.

The children's first attempts generally included ideas that the battery was the source of power, the light bulb the object, and the wire some type of connector to the object.

Mr. Clark used questions like, "How many ways can you light the bulb?" to promote observation and to encourage testing of student ideas. He encouraged the children to note which parts of the battery and bulb were "hooked up" in each of their trials, especially when they managed to light the bulb. Mr. Clark knew that the following issues would need to be dealt with as the first few teams discovered a solution:

1. *The solution would spread like wildfire throughout the classroom and be copied by other students. While this in itself is a powerful learning tool because it allows children to "get off the starting block" at about the same time, Mr. Clark wisely threw out another challenge so that the children who finished first still had much to do. In searching for multiple ways to light the bulb all students were treated to the discovery that there was not only one right answer. When they looked at each team report, they noticed some regularities, some things that worked, and others that did not. They also were surprised to find that some strategies they thought would work did not.*

2. *Some of the successes were due to chance. Perhaps a student used the rim of the battery instead of the top or bottom—on some batteries that will work just as well as connecting the wire to the bottom. The bulb lit unexpectedly. So careful observation and drawings as a means of communication needed to be encouraged.*

Recognizing these two issues, Mr. Clark really needed to pose questions as he went along. Asking how many ways students could light the bulb enticed students to be creative. Once they had learned the overriding principle of circuits, they might be more creative than they would have been in a more traditional experiment. For instance, students have been known to take off the metal jacket on the battery to discover that the zinc "innards" anywhere on the sides of the battery work just as well as the bottom. With this lesson, Mr. Clark made it possible for students to forget the "one right answer" approach of most problem-solving efforts. The result was myriad creative tries—some that worked, others that didn't. The more successes students experienced, the more they tried to find other ways to light the bulb.

Being successful at lighting the bulb was only one part of the process of developing the concept of a circuit. Mr. Clark knew that students needed to hone their model by proposing explanations *and* solutions *to the concept they were constructing. Additionally, the principle of the circuit as part of a system needed to be developed. This was done by integrating the concept of circuit as a system into a set of words that could be used to communicate ideas about systems and extend those ideas to other, more compli-cated circuits. When Mr. Clark and his students reviewed all of the reports, isolated the ways that worked, and tried to figure out why some strategies failed, they were on their way to a more scientifically correct understanding of circuits.*

The students needed to articulate *their findings for themselves and to others. Mr. Clark had students duplicate their solutions with the same materials and instructed the teams to carefully draw a model and then write down what they had observed about the successful model. If they needed words to describe what they had done, he suggested some.*

From looking at their work and that of others, Mr. Clark's student teams noticed regularities—patterns—that would predict whether a bulb would light or not. From these regularities, student teams would articulate the rules they observed. This process took several class periods to accomplish. When they were finished, every student understood the concept of a circuit, could call it by name, and could infer from a diagram if a circuit was complete.

If Mr. Clark had not refined his inquiry-discovery approach, only some of his students would have achieved the conceptual learning outlined above, and fewer would have been able to put the concept of circuit into the larger conceptual picture of systems. And if traditional teaching techniques had been used—if Mr. Clark had merely demonstrated how circuits are made—students may have learned one way of lighting the bulb and some textbook definitions of the parts of a circuit, and most would have forgotten the vocabulary very quickly. They would have been robbed of the excitement of finding out for themselves and forfeited the intrigue of discovering that circuits can be made in at least four different ways—sometimes even six or more, depending on how adventuresome they were and how tolerant Mr. Clark was. Most important, they likely would have failed to construct a mental model of the circuit, and their ability to apply the concept to other situations or diagrams would have been quite limited.

TAKING ACTION ON WHAT WE KNOW

How can schools adopt the effective instructional model presented in this chapter? For starters, educators at all levels need to be aware of instructional models that foster higher order thinking and concept development through constructivist learning. It is not enough to encourage all teachers to be process-oriented. There must be opportunities for teachers to learn how to introduce and exploit exploratory activities within the instructional model proposed here. School administrators need to lend their support and reward teachers who are taking risks to use these practices. Administrators need to know good science teaching when they see it, given their roles as evaluators and instructional leaders. Sufficient implementation and follow-up time are needed to help teachers make the significant changes involved. Teachers need support that will enable them to feel good about taking the time to learn and use the teaching techniques used by Ms. Lopez and Mr. Clark.

LOCAL ROLES

Things to do now:

1. **Involve key players**—administrators, principals, teachers, parents, the community—in developing and promoting an instructional model that promotes the same mechanism that scientists use to do science.

2. **Work with teachers to evaluate materials currently in use** to determine how (or if) they can be used in this model. Where, for example, do the current textbooks fit?

Things to do for the future:

1. **Make available materials that support the adopted instructional model.** (See descriptions of new materials in the Models and Resources section of this chapter for more detail.)

2. **Identify or develop staff development resources that help teachers adopt the instructional model** by structuring an ongoing inservice program that allows teachers to experience, understand, and practice it, as well as to be coached in actually using it. The training should include cooperative learning, questioning techniques, assessment in the service of instruction, and the role of teacher as facilitator. Administrators can promote this by recognizing teachers who become co-learners with students. Create the expectation that all teachers who have been trained to use the model will do so.

3. **Institute a support system**, like peer coaching, where teachers work together to look at their successes and difficulties with the new instructional model. The nature of support will need to change over time. Initial support, for example, might address issues such as teacher concern over proposed instructional changes. Later on, support efforts could focus on managerial tasks and implications for student needs.

4. **Design assessment strategies** that match and support the adopted model of instruction. These might include portfolios of children's work, documentation of systematic observations of children's performance, and notes from discussions with individuals or groups of children.

5. **Manage curriculum and materials** in districts so that they match and support the adopted instructional model. In addition

to appropriate materials, provide for a petty cash fund to facilitate use of the model, especially for some instances of "taking action" where students may need to do things like send letters about an environmental issue to the mayor.

6. **Arrange partnerships** with labs, universities, or science-oriented business firms. Visits by students or by their staff to classrooms can bring science to life, helping children see how scientists and engineers go about their work.

STATE ROLES

Things to do now:

1. **Institute staff development initiatives** that train teachers about the how and why of using an instructional model that promotes high-level conceptual development. Gear the training toward the philosophy of teachers as facilitators of knowledge. Make sure that staff development covers use of strategies like questioning techniques, cooperative learning, learning style awareness, and assessment in the service of instruction.

2. **Convey expectations and support of excellence in science education to faculty and parents.** This means public support for effective instructional models that emphasize more in-depth exploration of concepts rather than covering a multitude of topics superficially. If effective, this should lessen the pressure on teachers to finish the science textbook by the end of the school year.

3. **Incorporate the adopted instructional model into state curriculum guidelines.** Curriculum must be linked closely to an instructional model, otherwise there is a risk that teachers will teach but students will not learn—at least in the sense that we have presented in this chapter. Without this linkage, students may, at best, only memorize information without understanding it.

Things to do for the future:

1. **Encourage college and university programs to introduce instructional models** that help prospective teachers learn teaching methods that parallel the scientific investigative process.

2. **Recommend that college and university programs** develop undergraduate science courses that employ an instructional

model that corresponds to how scientists do science. If such courses were to use the model discussed in this chapter, teachers would have experienced good teaching for themselves, unlike current practice.

MODELS AND RESOURCES

A Model Curriculum: *Improving Urban Elementary Science*, a curriculum currently under development by the Education Development Center (EDC), uses an instructional-learning framework similar to the one in this chapter. The framework guides learners through four phases: getting started, experiencing and discovering, processing for meaning, and extending ideas.

A Model Curriculum: *Science for Life and Living: Integrating Science, Technology, and Health* is currently under development by the Biological Sciences Curriculum Study (BSCS). It incorporates a five-step instructional-learning model—engagement, exploration, explanation, elaboration, and evaluation—compatible with the model described in this chapter.

A Model Curriculum: The National Science Resources Center at the Smithsonian Institution is currently developing a curriculum entitled Science and Technology for Children, which promotes an inquiry-oriented teaching model similar to the one proposed in this chapter.

A Center: The Center for Teaching Thinking at The Regional Laboratory for Educational Improvement for the Northeast and Islands in Andover, Massachusetts, specializes in infusing the teaching of thinking across the curriculum. The Center provides training, assistance, materials, and other resources to educators throughout the country.

Key References

Bybee, R. W., C. E. Buchwald, L. S. Crissman, D. Heil, P. J. Kuerbis, C. Matsumoto, and J. D. McInerney. (1989). *Science and Technology Education for the Elementary Years: Frameworks for Curriculum and Instruction*. Andover, Mass.: The National Center for Improving Science Education, The NETWORK, Inc.

Dunn, K., and R. Dunn. (1987). "Dispelling Outmoded Beliefs about Student Learning." *Educational Leadership* 44, 6: 55-62.

Hawkins, D. (1983). "Nature Closely Observed." *Daedalus* 112: 65-90.

Johnson, D., and R. Johnson. (1987). *Learning Together and Alone: Cooperative, Competitive and Individualistic Learning*. Englewood Cliffs, N.J.: Prentice-Hall.

Novak, J. (1988). "Learning Science and the Science of Learning." *Studies in Science Education* 77-101.

Resnick, L. (1983). "Toward a Cognitive Theory of Instruction." In *Learning and Motivation in the Classroom*, edited by S. Parls, G. Olson, and H. Stevenson. Hillsdale, N.J.: Erlbaum.

Swartz, R. (1989). *Critical Thinking*. Addison-Wesley Science Professional Information Bulletin. Menlo Park, Calif.: Addison-Wesley.

Swartz, R. (In press). "Structured Teaching for Critical Thinking and Reasoning in Standard Subject Area Instruction." In *Informal Reasoning and Education*, edited by J. Voss, D. Perkins, and J. Segal. Hillsdale, N.J.: Erlbaum.

Tobin, K. (November 1988). "Learning in Science Classrooms." Paper presented at the Biological Sciences Curriculum Study 30th Anniversary Symposium on Curriculum Development for the Year 2000, Colorado Springs, Colo.

7.
Assess What
Is Valued

Do we assess what we value? Not really. We tend to
test what is easiest to measure: factual knowledge.
Testing what we value—a full understanding of
science knowledge and the ability to apply it,
problem-solving and thinking skills, and a positive
attitude toward science—is a much taller order. To
meet the goal of scientific literacy, we must start
testing what really matters.

WHAT WE KNOW

Many factors covered elsewhere in this book—time, teachers'
basic science knowledge, lack of exemplary teaching materials and
training—interfere with the teaching of what we say we value in
science education. And this discrepancy between what we say and
what we do is even greater when it comes to assessment. What
results is a sizable assessment challenge.

To deal with this challenge, we first need to address the
discrepancy between what we say we value in science education and what we teach. Indeed, ask teachers and administrators
at the elementary level what should be taught in science, and they
will often instinctively answer, "knowledge, skills, and attitudes."
However, a quick look at their curriculum would most likely reveal
a textbook-driven focus on the traditional content of facts and
names. Moreover, other valued outcomes—like concept development and the ability to apply science knowledge, practice a variety

of science process skills, and develop scientific attitudes—somehow get lost in the "make sure to cover all of the important facts" shuffle. Yet these broader outcomes *must* be addressed if we are to remain serious about developing scientific and technological literacy and achieving our long-term national goals for science education at all grade levels.

Likewise, there is a discrepancy between what we say we value and what we assess, despite the growing consensus of teachers, districts, and states about what's really important in science education. Think back to almost every science test you've ever taken. What do you remember? Most of us visualize a sea of multiple-choice questions that probed for scientific facts. These recall tasks had little relation to our daily lives, *nor* to scientific literacy. In all likelihood, they did not analyze and test for important facts and concepts, much less for thinking and problem-solving skills.

Things haven't changed that much. Teachers' tests still tend to be saturated with items that merely require factual recall. Such methods are the favored assessment choice for many reasons: (1) a "right answer/wrong answer" mentality, which makes measurement easy; (2) not knowing alternatives to the right/wrong approach and needing to base grades on *something*; (3) fat textbooks, an already crowded curriculum, and multiple-item, quick-answer tests that compete for teaching time; (4) inadequate preparation for teaching and assessing science; and (5) limited resources: time, energy, and funds.

> If we consider how many "right" answers are awarded because of a good guess or incorrect assumption, or, even worse, the number of "wrong" answers tallied because of knowing too much about a given topic, we are compelled to think again about employing right/wrong answer approaches to assessment.

To declare, however, that all science tests are simply designed to probe for trivia is to denigrate the efforts of hard-working, overworked teachers. Perhaps we need to step back and ask if what is currently assessed *is* what is valued by teachers and students alike. Can we assume that the omitted outcomes are not important to them? Indeed, **many of our assessment problems are a result of how science is perceived by the public and by teachers.** We tend to teach how we've been taught. Stereotypes persist in science—the imprint on our brain stubbornly insists that facts and figures *are* science. The problem inherent in this notion is the continual explosion of new knowledge—that there is simply too much knowledge to cover it all in the limited amount of time allocated to science, nor should we even try. In fact, the stereotype supports our contention that it's much more important to teach and test the major concepts, themes, and skills of science, and the relationship of science and technology to our daily lives.

The bottom line is that **assessment that leans heavily on fact regurgitation does little to foster the other things we value:** understanding of scientific concepts and of the ways scientific inquiry responds to questions about the world around us, the ability and disposition to use problem-solving skills, and the clarity to appreciate and pull from the shelves of our minds what is learned in science for use in our daily lives. We need to continue to work within the constraints of our particular system to improve our assessment strategies.

> Although there is broad consensus that scientific and technological literacy for all citizens is highly valued, the direction of most assessment efforts to date has not reinforced this value.

TAKING ACTION ON WHAT WE KNOW

How can we begin to effectively assess what we value? By using assessment tools that measure:

- *Factual and conceptual knowledge,* including:
  - facts about the child's immediate natural world, like knowing that the moon passes through cycles and about electrical circuits, disease, and nutrition;
  - knowledge about technology, like gears and pulleys, the development of health care systems, and the design of various inventions like a device to collect seeds;
  - concepts that scientists use to explain observations about the natural world, like how an animal's structures are related to the particular structure's function and how a simple machine is an example of a system; and
  - knowledge about the scientific venture, its philosophy as a way of knowing, and its history, like the evolution of

the view that the earth was the center of the universe to our present concept of the solar system.

- *Skills* inherent in doing science in the classroom, including:
  — use of the tools of science, learned through science laboratory activities, like focusing a telescope on the moon and weighing objects with an equal-arm balance;
  — intellectual skills used in applying the methods of science, like the ability to develop a hypothesis about the moon's phases; to design an experiment that is a valid test of that hypothesis; and to collect, produce, analyze, and present data; and
  — the general thinking skills used in reasoning and problem solving in science, like considering how to clean up an oil spill and determining which brand of paper towel is a better buy.

- The development of a variety of *attitudes* related to science, including:
  — scientific "habits of mind," like skepticism, tolerance of ambiguity, and respecting reason; and
  — positive attitudes toward science, which will lead to a willingness to apply science knowledge and science-based skills outside the classroom.

Is it really possible to assess this wide a variety of outcomes? Here's an example of how Ms. Lopez did so in her seeds unit:

Ms. Lopez had many opportunities for evaluating growth of understanding for individual students or groups of students. Each student gave an oral presentation about a seed she had found and examined; participated in a group that was asked to write, graph, or confer with Ms. Lopez; and shared in whole-class activities in which each student question or statement was an indication of progress (or lack of progress). Ms. Lopez was interested in several different types of understanding: Did the children develop an understanding of the role of seeds and their various properties in propagating plants and in providing food for animals and humans? More important, did they develop an understanding of some of the nine organizing concepts that had been illustrated through the study of seeds? Were they more adept at using a lens and at measuring length, weight, and volume? And did they develop some sense of systematic observation, recording, and analysis of data as they collected seeds, organized their collection, and germinated the seeds?

> What if language arts assessment *ended* with learning to identify the letters of the alphabet? Students acquired the factual knowledge, but to what end?

Note that in this definition of what we value, testing for knowledge means more than testing only for disconnected facts, as illuminated by our alphabet example. When we start to ask, "What purpose can there be in testing only for facts?" we will conclude that there is little purpose. Facts will remain forever lost in the crevices of our minds unless we connect them to meaningful concepts. The problem is exacerbated by the ease, simplicity, and efficiency with which knowledge of facts can be assessed. Many, perhaps most, assessment efforts unfortunately end there. Adequate assessment of the other outcomes may require observation, open-ended responses, and testing items that allow multiple answers—assessment techniques that are explored in Chapter 9.

LOCAL ROLES

Things to do now:

1. **Clarify the most valued goals.** Carefully define the overarching goals that are most valued for each grade level to delineate a framework for *what* should be assessed. When completed, share the framework with school and district personnel—curriculum directors, principals, science specialists, teachers—who can then be helped to plan, teach, and assess programs with the new framework in mind. Also inform parents, school boards, and the local community of the rationale behind the new direction in assessment.

2. **Determine whether or not current assessment practices measure identified goals and values for science education.** Before even beginning this task, examine the curriculum to ensure that the valued content is there in the first place. (See Chapters 2 through 4.) Analyzing assessment practices for whether they mea-

sure depth of knowledge, usable skills, critical thinking skills, positive attitudes, and meaningful application can then follow.

3. Encourage teachers to think of assessment as an ongoing process, part of their instruction: It is a guide both to their own instruction and to their students' understanding of what they are learning.

Things to do for the future:

1. Develop or adopt assessment techniques that match what is valued in science learning and that reinforce the goals of science education. For example:

- Assess knowledge through techniques that probe for depth of understanding of facts, concepts, and the ability to use problem-solving skills.

- Assess skills through hands-on performance tasks in which student competencies and reasoning skills become apparent.

2. Set aside time for developing techniques that really do assess what we value. The prevailing philosophy is that such development can be squeezed in after school or during the summer. But this task will require more than a casual effort. Careful thought and working on the issues a few at a time can contribute to success.

3. Raise the education and larger community's awareness of the problems with traditional tests and of issues in the comparison of test scores. Make a case for the usefulness of alternative perspectives and strategies for assessment, demonstrating whenever possible.

> By making a concerted, continuous effort, schools, principals, and teachers can begin to employ the type of assessment strategies that will assess what is valued.

STATE ROLES

Things to do now:

1. Incorporate all of the dimensions of science that are valued—depth of knowledge, science process and general thinking skills, and positive attitudes—**into statewide assessment tools and efforts.** Good assessment strategies at the state level are paramount because they tend to drive local science programs and local assessment. If states stop at assessing only factual knowledge, teachers and schools notice, and there is little incentive to focus on other valued outcomes. By acknowledging a broader view of assessment, states can motivate local pioneers to follow their lead, since no system wants to come up short by doing poorly.

2. Support local school districts to clarify what they value and to design assessment strategies that are parallel. This can best be achieved through a combination of clear expectations and direction—and enough assistance to do the job well. This assistance can include institutes for learning about and developing assessment strategies, test banks, and other help to promote successful local efforts.

MODELS AND RESOURCES

Assessment practices are still in their infancy. We are only now beginning to realize the potential effectiveness of assessment as a tool for examining long-term student progress, providing important insight into how students think, and illustrating how they engage in science. It is therefore not surprising that few well-tested assessment models exist that we can recommend as exemplary. There are, however, some prototypes that have been tried at the time of this writing. Two of these are major efforts by a local district and a state education agency to build assessment tools that measure what they value for elementary school science. While characterized by the agencies as program evaluations, some of their activities appear to be adaptable for the elementary classroom.

A Local Model: In spring 1988, the science department of the Minneapolis Public Schools conducted an assessment of the K-6 science program. Testing in 15 classrooms in 14 schools, 410 students took part. The purpose of the assessment was to test whether the existing curriculum builds, as it is intended to, a set of experiences that form the basis of concept development and teach the process skills necessary for investigation and experimentation, and to what extent it promotes students' confidence in their ability to do science.

The content and process portions of the test were given using a paper-and-pencil format and were administered to students individually. Approximately half of the students took each form of the laboratory test. This test was administered in student pairs to gather information about the students' ability to observe and describe objects and events, classify objectives, and perform investigations. Students were divided among 12 stations and were rotated from station to station (hence the assessment's name: the Circus Model). At one station they observed a Cartesian diver and wrote down what they observed. At another, they classified pictures of dogs and justified their classification system. Another example of a station was a "feeling box," at which students were asked to describe a certain object among several in the box and explain what they thought it was made of.

Approximately 50 students were given an individually administered interview to assess their experimental design skills in a problem-solving setting. Students were shown two brands of paper towels and asked which of the two paper towels was best. They were then directed to select from the array of materials and supplies available and make a fair test to find the answer to the question. The interviewer coded the students' responses and behaviors with special attention to their ability to control variables.

Results of the assessment are available from the Minneapolis Public Schools.

A State Model: The New York State Department of Education is currently conducting a large-scale, statewide assessment of its K-4 science program with seven instruments, of which two are required. The first required instrument is a 45-item written test, which includes 29 multiple-choice items that focus on the principles of matter and 16 items that examine processes that can be assessed using paper and pencil. The second required instrument is a five-item, station-to-station, problem-solving performance test. The remaining instruments are an assessment of students' attitudes toward science, a classroom environment survey for students, and one survey each for teachers, principals, and parents and guardians.

The assessment effort is designed to (1) measure K-4 science learning, (2) tie assessment items to the state syllabus, and

(3) provide each school with an item analysis that identifies which science learning strategies are working well and which could be improved.

Two hundred thousand students participated in the first round of testing, which was completed in spring 1989. The sizable effort, particularly with respect to administering the performance test, was accomplished through a turn-key training program in which trainers at regional service centers (Board of Cooperative Educational Services) trained staff at each school. Results of the assessment are available from the department, which is also planning to disseminate the process through a systematic training program.

Key References

Educational Leadership 46, 7. (April 1989). Theme issue on "Redirecting Assessment."

Hein, G. E. (1987). "The Assessment of Science Learning in Materials-Centered Science Education Programs." *Science and Children* 25, 2: 8-12.

National Assessment of Education Progress. (1987). *Science Objectives: 1990 Assessment* (Booklet No. 21-3-10), and *Learning By Doing* (Report No. 17-HOS-80). Princeton, N.J.: Educational Testing Service.

Raizen, S. A., and J. S. Kaser. (May 1989). "Assessing Science Learning in Elementary School: Why, What, How?" *Phi Delta Kappan* 70, 9: 718-722.

Raizen, S. A., J. B. Baron, A. B. Champagne, E. Haertel, I. V. S. Mullis, and J. Oakes. (1989). *Assessment in Elementary School Science Education.* Andover, Mass.: The National Center for Improving Science Education, The NETWORK, Inc.

Yager, R. E. (October 1987). "Assess All Five Domains of Science." *The Science Teacher* 54: 33-37.

8.
Connect Curriculum, Instruction, and Assessment

Assessment can mean so much more than something teachers do to students at the end of a unit of study. A fuller picture would show assessment as a process that weaves like a thread through all phases—beginning, middle, and end—of student learning. We can learn to use assessment in the service of instruction when we deliberately connect it with teaching and learning, using assessment activities in ways that are indistinguishable from instruction.

WHAT WE KNOW

Authentic assessment of science learning is tied to curriculum and instructional goals. As true as this statement seems, it is far from a reality in most science programs. Part of the reason lies in the external measures of science learning—benchmark tests, state-mandated tests, and state and local assessments—that continually barrage schools and teachers. It's not uncommon for schools and states to judge the quality of their entire science program on one or two external measures like the SAT and the Iowa Test of Basic Skills. This practice promotes a vicious cycle in which **teachers and schools, consciously or not, tailor their curriculum to what is tested, instead of the other way around. And because factual knowledge without conceptual understanding is the focus of what is typically measured by standardized tests, curriculums lack the other things we value: concept development, science process and thinking skills, and scientific attitudes.**

To promote these valuable goals of science education, **future assessment efforts will need to use strategies that measure the attainment of them.** Data from a fuller assessment effort can then be used to help redesign science curriculums and instruction that are more congruent with intended outcomes. Here assessment becomes a tool for broadening rather than narrowing the scope of the curriculum. It supports evolving, not stagnant, classroom activities that highlight important ideas, concepts, skills, and relationships. It also allows for matching curriculum to the strengths and problems of a particular community or region, thereby increasing the appropriateness of science for all students.

> Reforms in assessment in Great Britain reflect this broader view of testing. Their system addresses both the *improvement* of instruction and the need to tie assessment to instruction.

Our model builds on a view of continuous assessment using strategies that help teachers monitor the full range of student learning and adjust instruction accordingly. This means:

• **Student competence to perform science-related skills is assessed through hands-on activities,** such as finding an object's mass, determining which paper towel is the most absorbent, or predicting which substance—a piece of wax paper or plastic wrap—supports the largest amount of water.

• **Teacher questions that require students to justify and defend, two important science thinking skills,** play a role in good assessment. For instance, in a class where students have been comparing seedlike objects and real seeds, the teacher might give students Redhot candies (which look like small red seeds) and ask that they be placed in either the seed pile or nonseed pile. Students are then asked to produce a convincing argument to justify and support their decision.

• **There is value in considering how a student approaches an assessment task, how a hands-on activity was carried out, or how an answer was obtained—as well as the product of that assessment: the correctness of the answer.** Focusing on the *process* yields a world of information about how children think. Reflect on this example:

A group of children were shown pictures with stick figures pointing in different directions: up, down, and sideways. They were asked to indicate which figure pointed to the earth. A number of children chose the figure that pointed directly ahead. Asked why, they said that trees, houses, and people are all part of the earth. Those who indicated that the earth was above them said that they were not sure where the earth stopped! Yet another surprise came when some of those who chose the right answer, the figure pointing at the ground, said they chose it because the ground was dirt and that dirt and earth were the same.

The right answer/wrong answer assessment mode seems less useful as we learn how kids formulate their answers. Yes/no and multiple-choice items provide no insight into how children approach a problem, whether they are relying on rote memory, or if they really understand the *concept* behind the question. Indeed, note the wealth of information the teacher would have missed had he stopped with a single answer for the question above. We need to ask: What is most important in assessment? Are we only rewarding students who are adept at memorization? In the example above, might it be worthwhile to base assessment on which student provided the most thoughtful answer, rather than merely the right one?

• **Good assessment exercises are indistinguishable from instructional tasks.** Review the example below and ask whether a clear line can be drawn between the assessment and instructional activities in Ms. Lopez's class.

Ms. Lopez was almost finished with her unit on seeds. After observing many objects, some seeds and some not, students compiled the following list of characteristics that had to exist for an object to be called a seed:

1. It would grow if planted in the right environment.
2. It always contained a baby plant.
3. It always had a skin over the outside.

4. *It could either be like corn, one solid unit with a baby plant on one side, or it could be like a bean, two halves with a baby plant in between.*
5. *It can't be black. (They were convinced that there were no black seeds.)*
6. *There was a whitish spot on one end.*

On the day Ms. Lopez was to complete the lesson, John brought a small piece of a blue plastic berry basket to class. John stated emphatically, "This is a seed. It's one piece, like corn. See, it has skin." (He peels a small piece of plastic from the surface.) "It's not black and it has a spot on one side. See the bump? That's the baby plant."

After much discussion, the class decided to plant the blue "seed." John observed, "This seed is like an acorn; it will take about six weeks to sprout, and school will be over by then."

One by one, the students reviewed everything they ever knew about seeds, and the plastic berry fragment fit the model they had painstakingly constructed. Finally, in desperation, the class decided to burn the "seed" to see if it smelled like burning seed or plastic. Ms. Lopez, glad to oblige, suggested that not all plastic, or for that matter, seeds may smell alike when burned. However, an experiment was planned and executed, and John's seed indeed had a burning plastic smell anyone could recognize.

Clearly, Ms. Lopez was able to assess knowledge, skills, and scientific habits of mind more effectively during this exchange than if she had given the students a traditional paper-and-pencil test. By having to justify their conclusions, her students were forced to reexamine their seed model. In the end, they had to design a fair test for a hypothesis and alter their model based on the test results.

This is what good science assessment is really about: measuring depth of understanding as well as simple mastery of knowledge, using a variety of formal and informal techniques.

Future assessments will be conceived as an ongoing, cyclical process in which assessment feeds, informs, shapes, and improves curriculum and instructional decisions.

TAKING ACTION ON WHAT WE KNOW

How can we adopt this new model of assessment? What needs to happen? **First, we ought to help teachers and administrators view assessment as something that includes, but goes beyond, testing of factual information.** Second, we need to embrace the notion that the primary role of assessment is to inform teacher decision making for both curriculum and instruction. This will require continually gathering assessment information that would be routinely and seriously considered in decision making.

Next, reinforce the fact that assessment can better improve and be tied to instruction when it is used for a variety of purposes, including:

• **Assessing student understanding before, during, and after instruction.** Assessing students' prior knowledge and skills **before instruction** demonstrates the conceptions students bring with them and sets the stage for future learning activities. What—if any—misconceptions to dispel, which instructional strategies to choose, how best to group students during team learning, and what laboratory or hands-on skills have already been mastered are important pieces of information to gather before instruction begins. Here is how Ms. Lopez did this:

Before beginning the seeds unit, Ms. Lopez had invited the class to talk about seeds by asking: "What are some examples of seeds?" The children were eager to contribute ideas and called out many. She mentally noted which of the children hung back—some might be shy; some might be unsure of what a seed is. Later, she would find other, unobtrusive ways to probe the understanding of some of these children individually.

She noted something interesting about the set of answers the students had given: They seemed to associate seeds with things they ate. She thought she could build on that when she was ready to introduce the idea of seeds as having concentrated energy to help plants grow. The children also seemed to associate seeds with plants. But their conception of seeds had limitations. The teacher made a mental note to bring a coconut, a pine cone, and some peppercorns to school.

When the 15-minute activity was finished, Ms. Lopez had done several things: She knew what the children understood in a general way, and she had some ideas about which ones might require some extra help later on. She also perceived which children seemed to have a lot of ideas, and later, when the children would work in small groups, she would try to have each group include one of these children. She had identified some "hooks" to the children's own understandings and experiences that she could capitalize on later. All this, and the children didn't even know it was an assessment!

During instruction, students' adeptness at carrying out activities, understanding of major scientific concepts, and individual progress, as well as general needs, can all be determined. Teacher assessment strategies may include systematic student observation, asking probing questions, listening to small-group discussions, and reviewing student journals and write-ups of observations and procedures. Low student understanding, poor skill development, and persistent misconceptions are all signals for teachers to reinforce instruction with alternative methods. For example:

After several weeks of working with seeds, Ms. Lopez wants to assess whether the children have developed good ideas about testing factors that are important in plant germination and growth. As the children set up various conditions, she notes that some are having difficulty weighing soil and solid fertilizer and measuring water and liquid fertilizer. She takes time to work with the children on these skills until they have mastered them.

After instruction, when most attempts at assessment begin and end, three well-conceived strategies can be used: (1) performance-based activities in which individual students or working groups are asked to perform tasks that employ skills and concepts they should have learned, (2) paper-and-pencil tests that require students to justify answers and develop convincing arguments for particular points of view, and (3) more standard multiple choice and essay examinations, which are valid and useful, especially when used with other assessment techniques.

• **Motivating students and (re)defining student roles.** Even simple assessment strategies, like asking intriguing questions, can work to motivate kids to want to learn more. Effective assessment may also help teachers cast roles for students in cooperative work groups. As students deal with provocative scientific problems in such groups, they will be even more motivated and productive. And isn't motivation for learning one of the true benefits of students taking responsibility for their own learning?

• **Communicating and documenting.** Communicating to students their teachers' expectations about what is to be learned, and sharing with parents and the greater community the documented results of what was gained through the science program, are but two examples of how assessment can serve as an ideal vehicle for communication.

In the classroom, good assessment can be a powerful tool for focusing instruction and providing information to both teachers and students about learning progress. Incorporating assessment into instruction in thoughtful ways can provide teachers with the feedback needed to help their students and to communicate with others. Following is one example of such practice.

Students were asked to keep a journal noting physical and behavioral characteristics of crayfish. Observations, along with other information from reference materials, were used to create "the life story" of a crayfish. The teacher periodically read the students' journals and could follow up with feedback on what areas they still needed to work on.

Outside of the classroom, the results of assessment can be highlighted to convey the benefits of useful information learned and skills gained, which ultimately serves to promote the importance of science education for the general well-being of society.

> State and national efforts should provide teachers with the necessary skills and time to design and implement assessment models that use good science teaching techniques such as hands-on activities. Using assessment in this manner would result in dramatic change in elementary science programs.

LOCAL ROLES

Things to do now:

1. **Involve teachers and administrators** in all stages of goal setting, assessment development, and subsequent evaluation of assessment results.

2. **Provide inservice programs that help teachers re-examine their assessment techniques.** Help them develop the neces-

sary skills and attitudes to implement the type of assessment strategies advocated in this book. Focus attention on improving the kinds of curriculum-embedded and teacher-constructed tests most often used in the classroom. Use a set of questions such as those on page 102 of Chapter 9 to help teachers analyze their tests. Use other assessment checklists, such as those developed by some states and by the National Science Teachers' Association, to look at what is taught and how it is measured (see Key References at the end of Chapter 10). Many of these devices also enable curriculum developers, curriculum coordinators, and classroom teachers to get help in assessing outcomes that are not covered by conventional testing procedures.

Consider offering the following staff development opportunities:

- A "how to" session on connecting assessment to curriculum and instruction; offer it as an inservice, but also use the information when developing curriculum guides, scope and sequence, or working with teachers to design science activities;

- Review the science learning process, with attention to an exemplary instructional model like the one proposed in Chapter 5 of this book, giving special emphasis to how teachers can and should evaluate student learning in a continuous manner.

3. Sensitize teachers to develop a fuller understanding of assessment by asking the following questions during routine supervisory conferences or in informal observation. Some questions might be: What were students learning? How did you know? Did you use information about what students were or were not learning to tailor instruction? How could you have done so?

Things to do for the future:

1. Move beyond curriculum guides that focus only on content. Though helpful, documents on what ought to be taught fall short of supporting effective assessment. Instead, develop guides that provide (1) recommendations that map out the overarching goals and objectives; (2) suggestions for how local districts can adapt, modify, or design their own goals; and (3) a plan that spells out the "how to's" of implementing an assessment cycle. Then use information gleaned from assessments to update the curriculum.

2. Help administrators alter a commonly held mindset that the textbook equals the curriculum. Give them opportunities to view curriculum development as a process that unfolds over the long term, relying on various methods of goal assessment as well as the informed judgment of staff members to determine science content and teaching methods.

3. Identify or develop assessment strategies based on curriculum and instructional strategies, such as cooperative learning, that tie nicely to assessment. This is not easy, so provide inservice opportunities to help teachers learn them well.

4. Research, identify, and disseminate effective testing practices that tie assessment to curriculum and instruction.

STATE ROLES

Things to do now:

1. Assume the role of trend setter by promoting assessment that informs curriculum and instruction. States should be sensitive, however, about getting too far ahead of their constituents. Districts may become overwhelmed by the sheer volume of work and either refuse to take action on new assessment recommendations or look for easy ways around them. To avoid this, look at the total curriculum structure as a cycle of planning, implementation, and assessment.

2. Seek input from classroom teachers, administrators, and representatives from higher education to decide on outcomes that must be achieved when students complete the K-12 sequence. These outcomes should form the core of the state's assessment model. Then make a commitment to an assessment effort that examines these valued outcomes and is also reflected in the state's curriculum framework.

3. Sponsor workshops, seminars, and other opportunities in which teachers, science supervisors, principals, and other local leaders can learn about and experiment with assessment models and strategies that link closely with curriculum and instruction. Assist them in implementing the models and strategies in their districts.

Things to do for the future:

1. **Publicize results of assessment efforts, not school by school, as some states have done, but by goals.** State and local leaders alike need to measure up to an assessment program driven by a broader set of goals. The high profile of state leadership can provide constructive pressure in setting a new direction in assessment.

2. **Establish a curriculum review cycle** to follow the progress of districts that have chosen to experiment with good assessment. Not only could this prove a useful evaluation of the effort for the districts, but it will produce models for consideration by other districts as well.

MODELS AND RESOURCES

A National or State Model: In Great Britain, assessment reforms address both the need for monitoring and improving instruction. Various instructional strategies include systematic teacher observation, student profiles over time, and structured tasks administered one-on-one or in small groups. The use of assessment strategies is accompanied by specific teacher training. (See Department of Education and Science and the Welsh Office 1987, and Woolnough and Allsop 1985, in Key References section.)

A Report: The National School Boards Association is currently finalizing a publication on assessment and its relationship to accountability. It promotes the need to look beyond standardized testing to other measures of school effectiveness and to consider different ways of reporting to the public. The report will discuss proposals of the National Assessment of Educational Progress, some state and local models, and implementation strategies for accurate accountability.

A State Model: Although focused on the secondary level, the Connecticut State Department of Education's efforts to develop a performance assessment are also of interest to elementary educators. The state is collaborating with other states as well to design a series of assessment tasks that will ask students to work individually and in groups to frame problems, collect data, and analyze and report their results. One goal of the assessment is to shift the emphasis in teaching from imparting facts to facilitating concept and skill development.

Key References

Department of Education and Science and the Welsh Office. (1987). *National Curriculum: Task Group on Assessment and Testing: A Report.* London: Her Majesty's Stationery Office.

Dowling, K. W. (1983). "Science Achievement Testing: Aligning Testing Method with Teaching Purpose." In *Students and Science Learning.* Washington, D.C.: AAAS.

Frederiksen, N. (1984). "The Real Test Bias: Influences of Testing on Teaching and Learning." *American Psychologist* 39: 193-202.

Hein, G., ed. (In press). *Assessment for Hands-on Science Programs.* Proceedings from 1989 Lesley College conference. Grand Forks, N.D.: North Dakota Study Group on Evaluation.

National Assessment of Educational Progress. (1987). *Science Objectives: 1990 Assessment* (Booklet No. 21-3-10) and *Learning By Doing* (Report No. 17-HOS-80). Princeton, N.J.: Educational Testing Service.

Raizen, S. A., J. B. Baron, A. B. Champagne, E. Haertel, I. V. S. Mullis, and J. Oakes. (1989). *Assessment in Elementary School Science Education.* Andover, Mass.: The National Center for Improving Science Education, The NETWORK, Inc.

Woolnough, B. E., and T. A. Allsop. (1985). *Practical Work in Science.* Cambridge, England: Cambridge University Press.

9.
Use a Variety of Assessment Strategies

There is an endless variety of ways to assess science goals, most of them far superior to single-answer, paper-and-pencil tests. We must broaden our view of assessment and try other approaches if we truly want assessment to serve instruction.

WHAT WE KNOW

The last two chapters have set the stage: We need to assess what we value, and we need to tie assessment much more closely to curriculum and instruction. But how? Essentially through experimenting and selecting more thoughtfully among an array of alternative assessment strategies. We now need to ask, "Which assessment strategies further the types of curriculum and instruction that promote exemplary science learning?"

It is truly an exciting time to be talking about assessing science learning in elementary schools. Not only have we begun to reach consensus on the true goals of science education, but educators throughout the world are developing and experimenting with new and different ways to assess those goals. The fact that there is little research to confirm the value of one approach over another can be viewed in a positive light. It is *not* appropriate to apply pressure to teachers to use specific assessment strategies. Rather, it is a time to encourage exploration and experimentation and to engage educators at all levels in the effort.

Pushing beyond our confined image and practice of assessment reveals a wide array of possibilities:

Self-reports. Easy to design self-reports can be used for older elementary students as pre-tests to assess prior knowledge of a subject, concept, or process. They also help to develop students' ability for self-evaluation.

Multiple-choice tests with justification. Students indicate which answer they think is correct with a short justification explaining why.

Concept mapping. Students draw diagrams that illustrate connections, hierarchical relationships, and sequences. These can be used as either pre- or post-assessment tools.

Drawings. Students draw their perceptions and understandings of a particular learning. Drawings are a useful alternative for students who have difficulty with writing.

Problem analysis. Data and a problem to solve are presented to students, who attempt to describe and analyze the situation and offer explanations.

Research analysis. Students are presented with outlines of original research, which they are asked to analyze and evaluate.

Practical laboratory tests. Stations are set up with practical, hands-on tasks. Students can work alone, in pairs, or in groups to demonstrate skills and solve laboratory-related problems.

Games and simulations. Valid strategies for assessing student learning, these techniques are interesting and fun, and they sometimes help students forget that they are learning in the process.

Testing outdoors. Like testing for lab skills, testing outdoors serves as a vehicle for testing real understanding of environmental phenomena.

Computer-based assessment. Computers are important tools that are now being used for assessment as well as instruction.

Other tests. Take-home tests, cooperative tests, assignments to make or construct something, and open-book tests are but a few examples of alternatives to traditional testing.

And we needn't feel limited to *formal* assessment approaches. Informal approaches have also been used successfully to assess science learning. *Methods of informal assessment* include teacher observations of student work, their participation in both large-and small-group discussions, and how they set up and conduct experiments. Profiles of student performance over time can be developed with data gathered from a variety of sources. Student journals can be used to reveal much about their thinking and their development of knowledge, skills, and attitudes.

With such an interesting array of formats, the compelling question becomes, "What can best be assessed in which ways?" Assessing knowledge requires somewhat different choices than assessing science skills, and assessing attitudes and scientific habits of mind still others. What do we know about how to make appropriate choices?

Assessing Knowledge

Knowledge is the easiest goal to measure, and it's the assessment task teachers generally feel most comfortable with. Assessing knowledge usually entails making a decision about which categories of science knowledge to measure and then selecting specific information to be represented on a test. Tests for knowledge have the advantage that they can be administered easily, with paper and pencil, to groups of children. Further, if the items are well constructed, they can be interpreted with reasonable certainty. A correct answer indicates that either the student knew what was required for the answer or was able to figure it out, given the information.

Assessing knowing in this way does not have to be restricted to memorizing factual information for regurgitation on a test. Here is an example:

Which of the following is not a seed? Why?

a. nut
b. pebble
c. egg
d. acorn

Here, an understanding of the concept of seed is required to respond to the "why" question, although making the correct choice may be relatively easy.

Multiple-choice test questions are here to stay, given their usefulness in assessing some kinds of knowledge. Elementary teachers, though, aren't as compelled to use multiple-choice tests as secondary teachers or those conducting large-scale testing.

Because they have fewer students, elementary teachers have the opportunity to go beyond multiple-choice testing and make assessments more useful for their teaching.

There are some ways, however, recognizing their limitations, that we can continue to use multiple-choice tests and at the same time move in the direction of more valuable assessment. Pincus Tamir, of the Hebrew University in Jerusalem, has explored an interesting variety of paper-and-pencil tests to assess different outcomes. In his manuscript, "Innovative Testing in Science" (undated), Tamir presents some useful suggestions along with commonsense approaches for improving multiple-choice assessment. Specifically, he looks at the issue of why students choose one answer over another—the rationale behind their decisions. He demonstrates how paying careful attention to three considerations can help turn multiple-choice questions into effective diagnostic tools.

1. Correct vs. Best Answers

Most multiple-choice tests are designed so that one option is correct and the remaining options—the distractors—are incorrect. This type of assessment requires little more than factual memorization. However, by asking students to choose the best rather than just the correct answer, they must carefully analyze the options presented and then select an answer that best fits the context and data given in the test item's stem. The process of choosing the best answer requires that students demonstrate a wide range of cognitive abilities. It also lets teachers look at *how* questions were answered—the reasoning behind students' choices—which, according to new research, may be even more important than selecting the correct answer. Let's look at the possibilities with a typical test item:

The dry weight of corn plants at the end of their growth is six tons per acre. All of this crop was produced from:

a. water and minerals absorbed from the soil (1)
b. minerals from the soil and oxygen from the air (13)
c. water and minerals from the soil and carbon dioxide from the air (64)
d. water, minerals and organic substances from the soil (22)

"C" is the best answer. The percentage of students who chose each option is shown in parentheses. If the open-ended question,

"How has all this crop been produced?" was asked instead, "by photosynthesis" would have been the correct answer. By employing the "best answer" approach, students needed to know that carbon dioxide from the air is a raw ingredient in photosynthesis, and to rule out the idea that plants absorb organic nutrients from the soil. Additionally, they needed to understand that the information in option (a) is not incorrect, but that it did not reflect the best answer to the question. The distribution of answers yields some interesting diagnostic information for the teacher: 22 percent of students think that plants get their organic matter from the soil and 13 percent confuse photosynthesis with respiration.

2. Construction of Diagnostic Multiple-Choice Items

Diagnostic multiple-choice items can be developed by using as distractors either known misconceptions or students' answers to open-ended questions. Many examples of students' misconceptions exist in the research literature (see Helm and Novak 1983) that would pass for excellent distractors for a variety of scientific topics. When there are none or not enough, teachers can collect answers to open-ended questions, analyzing them for patterns of fallacy. These can then be used on subsequent multiple-choice tests.

3. The Use of Justifications

A relatively small amount of research has been done on the use of justifications—in which students give reasons and arguments for the answers they chose—for multiple-choice tests. The reason for this is twofold: (1) Many educators avoid using justifications altogether because they negate the advantages associated with purely objective items, and (2) educators reason that justifications are the domain of essay questions. But there are several good reasons for using this approach with multiple-choice items: Justifications force students to seriously examine the data in each option, students will at least attempt to learn topics and concepts more deeply if they know they will have to justify their answers, and teachers will gain valuable insights into students' conceptions and reasoning patterns. In addition, research suggests that even for best-answer, multiple-choice assessment, many students still do not really understand the topic under study.

These are ways to improve on conventional methods for knowledge testing. But even more unconventional ways are called for if we are to see assessment as:

- Continuous rather than done only after a unit of study;
- Probing the depth and breadth of student understanding; and
- Providing opportunities for students to creatively apply their knowledge.

Diagnosing students' "entry position" for learning science is an important role for knowledge assessment. There are ways this can be done in an informal, yet valuable way—through teacher observation, for instance. Ms. Lopez probed her students' prior knowledge about seeds by asking the question, "What are some examples of seeds?" at the onset of the unit (see Introduction, pp. xv-xvii. She noted some interesting characteristics of the answers called out by students. The children associated seeds with plants and things they ate, for example. There were, however, limitations in their notions about seeds, and lots of reasons *why* students categorized one thing as a seed and not another. Ms. Lopez used these observations in future lessons. During her informal assessment activity, she also observed differences in the contributions made by individual children; these notes, too, were helpful in subsequent classes, especially in grouping the children.

Journals kept by students are an excellent way of tracking their development of scientific understanding over time. In one situation, students were instructed to observe their pets during a unit on animals and to make journal entries about what they saw. By checking student writing, the teacher easily noted which ones were paying attention to significant information and going on to make appropriate inferences about animals. The teacher could tell which students were learning about structure and function and about change—the two organizing concepts that the unit was focused on. Students who observed and discussed the cyclical nature of certain aspects of animal behavior were obviously using more developmentally complex forms of analysis than students who simply noted that their hamsters were brown.

This section has explored several ways of broadening our approach to knowledge assessment. But with a holistic view of the goals for elementary school science in mind, we also need to expand our concept of assessment to include a focus on skills and attitudes as well.

Assessing Laboratory Skills, Science Intellectual Skills, and Generic Thinking Skills

Assessing laboratory skills requires that the distinction be made between knowing about how to do something and actually being able to do it. To assess whether in fact children know how to do something—like find the mass of an object or the temperature of a liquid—requires that they be observed doing it. Thus skill assessment is inherently more complicated than knowledge assessment, particularly in terms of the logistics required to set up appropriate situations. Paper-and-pencil tests are a poor substitution; hands-on assessments are called for. In addition, students report that they enjoy practical tests and prefer them to paper-and-pencil approaches (Tamir undated).

> We have to think twice about producing students who can competently determine temperatures on a paper-and-pencil test but would fail at actually being able to use a mercury thermometer. Only through hands-on laboratory skill exercises can we assess the latter.

Measuring science intellectual skills and generic thinking skills poses an even greater challenge than testing for laboratory skill. Science intellectual skills require students not only to draw on a multitude of generic thinking skills, but also demands the capacity to *appropriately select* and perform lab skills, usually in the process of solving a problem. For example, when asked to find the mass of liquid contained in a beaker, the student needs to be a competent user of a balance and also must possess the thinking skills to design a suitable strategy to determine the mass of the liquid apart from its container.

If hands-on activities are the most appropriate way to assess mastery of certain skills, two basic assessment formats can be used. In individually administered assessments, students can (a) perform a specified task while an evaluator awards points against a prepared, competency-based checklist; (b) be interviewed with some predetermined questions, with additional questions being used to probe the thought process that produced the child's initial answer; or (c) undergo an oral examination using real-life situations or materials. Group-administered assessments are based on written responses from students who (a) are shown an experiment, set of materials, set of objects, and so on, and asked to do something with what they observe (e.g., predict, describe, explain); or (b) rotate from station to station in a laboratory setting, completing specified tasks.

The outdoors can provide an excellent environment for assessing skill development. Appropriate outdoor assessment activities might include observing differences between north- and south-facing slopes, examining brown spots and other unusual markings on plants, and observing the activity of honeybees or other insects or animals. However, the benefits of assessing from the real thing instead of models or makeshift environments in the classroom must be weighed against the discipline, organization, and control issues related to outdoor assessment. To facilitate a smooth operation, teachers can make a preparatory trip to the chosen site to catalog important phenomena. Logistics can be smoothed out in a variety of ways. For example, "stations" can be numbered and 3" x 5" cards used to give directions and pose questions to groups or to individual students.

Hands-on tasks can be used to assess skill development in many other ways. It is unfortunate that they are used so rarely. Because hands-on and field activities are so labor-intensive, paper-and-pencil activities are often substituted for them. By succumbing to easy assessment strategies, however, we run the risk of gathering misleading results. For example, in their program assessment using hands-on tasks, the Minneapolis public schools found that students able to read a stylized thermometer on a paper-and-pencil test often couldn't read a real thermometer. The New York State assessment had similar findings.

One labor-efficient strategy is to use reusable kits to conduct certain assessments. This saves teachers considerable time and effort. In addition, teachers can set up testing situations that address more than one skill, although it is important to observe a student closely to determine which skill(s) are lacking and obstructing the successful completion of the task, and which are not.

Skill assessment does not always have to occur in a formal setting. Informal assessments can occur during instruction as well, especially when students are engaged in hands-on activities. Teachers can make notes with anecdotal observations of student behavior, which they can use to monitor progress and skill development over time, as well as to adjust instruction.

Assessing Attitudes and Dispositions

In Chapter 4 we discuss the importance of developing in children positive dispositions toward science. In addition, we talk about the desirability of developing scientific habits of mind, such as:

- desiring knowledge
- being skeptical
- relying on data
- accepting ambiguity
- willingness to modify explanations
- cooperating in answering questions and solving problems
- respecting reason
- being honest

Assessing these attitudes, however, poses a sizable assessment challenge, one for which there are no readily available (or valid) approaches.

Probably the best way to assess attitudes is to observe student behavior over time (keeping informal records of student behaviors, responses, and remarks) and examining student choices and completed work for indicators. Pausing once in a while to answer questions such as the following can also provide information on student attitudes:

- Do students appear to enjoy developing methods for solving problems?
- Do students depend less on wild guesses and more on calculated estimations when faced with the kinds of large-number problems found in concept application?
- Do students appear to enjoy applying their estimating skills to computational problems in math?
- During discussions, are students able to offer their own ideas? Do they question other people's ideas as well as their own?
- Do students ask thoughtful and interesting questions related to the materials being studied?
- Do students smile when they are at work?

Beyond traditional knowledge assessment, what strategies did Ms. Lopez use to determine what students learned about seeds and how seeds grow? She assigned an ongoing performance activity in which students planted seeds and recorded their growth. They then weighed the pots and cooperatively decided how much soil to put in each (controlling variables). Students measured the height of their plants over time until all were more or less of uniform height, and they accounted for the amount of water each plant received. They then attempted to draw conclusions.

Throughout this process, Ms. Lopez had many opportunities to assess students, both formally and informally. For instance, she noted which students kept a journal, which groups made an attempt to compare their data with those gathered by other groups, and how well students understood the validity of their data and could account for the differences among group results. Ms. Lopez also noted which students learned weighing and measurement skills; she then went on to do more formal assessment of these skills by setting up practical lab tests in which students had to perform weighing tasks. She made opportunities for and observed her students' ability to talk about discrepant events—why one plant was short, wide, and green, while another was long, skinny, and yellow. She also checked on her students' ability to use language arts skills to describe procedures, observations, and conclusions as well as math skills to display data.

When the class moved on to similar challenges in its next unit, Ms. Lopez noted whether students were able to apply the knowledge and skills they had learned in the seeds unit. She noted their difficulties with perception and facts. By employing this comprehensive assessment strategy, Ms. Lopez was able to enrich the science curriculum and instruction as well as integrate language arts and mathematics with science without denigrating any one discipline.

TAKING ACTION ON WHAT WE KNOW

It's both limiting and unfortunate to view assessment as something that remains hidden in a closet until the end of a unit or, worse yet, the end of the year. Exemplary formal and informal assessment practices are *continuous*. Science leaders at both the state and local levels must start considering strategies for creating and supporting a continuous assessment cycle in classrooms. And assessment needs to be done for all the important goals of science—not only to find out what kids know, but to discover whether they can use the new information, how they think, and what attitudes and beliefs they hold about science and their ability to use it.

How can we promote the use of alternative assessment strategies? Before answering this question, let's acknowledge that, although some research is currently under way, we still do not have many real examples that can be advocated with surety. However, examples exist that have much promise and are worth pursuing. Also, uncertainty is not without merit; it's one of the characteristics that makes assessment an adventure for all educators. It's anybody's guess what assessment breakthroughs may lie around the corner. At the very least, *these strategies call for educators to become more sophisticated in their view of testing and assessment.*

The immediate issue is for science leaders to act on two major tasks. **First, we need to improve current assessment instruments so that they reflect the recommendations highlighted in this book.** Ask the following questions of current tests:

• Are there problems that require students to think about and analyze situations?

• Does the test feature sets of problems that call for more than one step in arriving at a solution?

• Are problems with more than one correct solution included?

• Are there opportunities for students to use their own data and create their own problems?

• Are students encouraged to use a variety of approaches to solve a problem? For example, at the initiation of the seed unit, Ms. Lopez might ask: "Where can we look for seeds to bring to class?"

• Are there assessment exercises that encourage students to estimate their answers and to check their results?

For science specifically, we would add:

• Is the science information given in the problem story and elicited in the answer accurate?

• Are there opportunities for assessing skills, both in the use of science tools and in science thinking, through exercises calling for hands-on activities?

• Are there exercises included in the overall assessment strategy that need to be carried out over time?

• Are there problems with purposely missing or mistaken information that ask students to find the errors or critique the way the problem is set up? (What is wrong? What is difficult?)

• Are there opportunities for students to make up their own questions, problems, or designs? For example, asking students to design a seed that has more than one dispersal feature (Raizen et al. 1989, p. 66).

Second, science leaders need to legitimize experimentation with a variety of alternative, informal assessment techniques. We need to promote informal assessment strategies that are both systematic (carried out on a regular basis) and comprehensive (covering all students)—not just random observations by teachers.

Teachers need to be given opportunities to carry out informal assessments on a regular basis with all students. Doing so will help to make informal assessments reliable because, just as with paper-and-pencil tests, replication breeds reliability. In addition, teachers will agree with the justifiability of informal assessment when they witness for themselves the powerful role it can play in the instructional decision-making process. For example, teachers can cull valuable information even from simple, quick, informal assessment like observing how well students respond to a problem-solving task. It's this kind of recognition that will help give informal assessment the legitimacy it deserves.

Teachers can use informal assessment findings for grading as well as communicating student progress to parents. Methods of informal record keeping and scoring might involve teachers preparing a file or record book that contains categories for a variety of valued competencies like information gathering, problem solving, and decision making capacity. Scoring systems and/or anecdotal entries can be set up for each category.

> Alternatives to traditional testing need to become an explicit part of assessing student achievement and progress, both in the classroom and for large-scale testing purposes.

However, we can't realistically expect teachers to seek out or develop new types of assessment when they have not been adequately prepared to do so. Preservice as well as inservice programs must be established to train and support teachers in developing a variety of formal and informal assessment tools.

For science educators, the conundrum is "Where do we start?" First, we need to acknowledge that individual schools constitute the basic unit for improving the assessment of science education goals within districts. Then go forth slowly, gradually looking beyond the paper-and-pencil tradition by experimenting with a few new assessment techniques. Make notes, adopt what works, discard what doesn't, and report back to state-level decision makers who need more local data to influence new directions in assessment. Although this advice sounds simplistic, districts and schools often attempt too much too quickly and, for lack of a readily apparent audience, keep the results to themselves.

LOCAL ROLES

Things to do now:

1. **Legitimize the use of a variety of assessment strategies to monitor the progress of science learning**. Send a clear message to teachers that it is not only okay to use forms of assessment other than paper-and-pencil, short-answer tests, but that a variety of assessment sources *should* be used. Teacher observation, when done systematically and comprehensively, is valid and important. These messages need to be sent to administrators and parents as well, so they begin to expect that student grades are based on more than test scores. Sponsor forums for parents and the community to talk about alternative assessment strategies.

2. **Encourage teachers to examine their current tests.** To do so, they can use criteria they develop themselves or the questions listed on page 102.

3. **Provide staff development opportunities in science assessment.** Action can't stop with the message, though. Teachers, administrators, and parents all need to learn about the why's and how's of good assessment, and they need to learn about different things in separate sessions. Teachers can benefit from seeing examples of diverse assessment approaches, understanding what makes them good, and working with their own curriculums to design alternative assessments. They especially need exposure to strategies for assessing goals other than knowledge, since these are rarely assessed. And they need to understand and practice informal assessment approaches that can make their collection of information more systematic and valid.

4. **Support both formal and informal assessment efforts of teachers in the elementary science program.** Teachers need support, time, and resources to employ the new types of assessments recommended in this guide. One way to support them is

by designing, with teacher assistance, assessment strategies that fit with the school or district science curriculum. Encourage teachers to work together to try out and refine their assessment strategies. Arrange for helpers when teachers want to use individual or small-group assessment strategies (these might be aides, parent or other volunteers, or high school science students). Convene informal discussion groups in which teachers bring their new assessment data to work together to understand what they are learning and how they can make their assessments more useful.

Things to do for the future:

1. Expand the district or school's approach to assessment through a gradual effort to add measures of goals other than knowledge and strategies that are informal in addition to formal. **Plan for the adoption of a variety of assessment strategies** that contribute to a profile of a student's progress, both within a grade and throughout his years in school.

2. Work with professionals at both the state and national levels to **develop and identify a variety of exemplary formal and informal assessment tools.** Provide opportunities for teachers to work with others outside the district to keep their vision of assessment current with a broadening national vision.

STATE ROLES

Things to do now:

1. Examine the tests given to students within the state. Establish your own criteria or use the list of questions on page 102.

2. Use available talent from local school districts, higher education, and other states to introduce science educators to alternative approaches to assessment. Set up institutes and forums to discuss the issues and learn what others are doing. Urge local districts to participate in an ongoing cycle of assessment planning, implementation, review, and renewal.

3. Grant waivers from the state science testing program (if one exists) to districts that want to experiment with alternative forms of assessment. Set up a mini-grant program to support experimentation, requiring clear documentation of what was done and with what results.

Things to do for the future:

1. Develop, identify, and make available to local districts a variety of exemplary informal and formal assessment approaches. It is essential that the approaches reflect current research and the full spectrum of assessment, including performance-based testing.

2. If a state testing program exists, expand it to incorporate strategies that assess the full range of science education goals.

MODELS AND RESOURCES

Although the movement to create alternative forms of assessment is growing, there are still few models that can be readily adopted. We note in Chapter 7 the efforts of the Minneapolis Public Schools and the New York State Department of Education. The hands-on performance portions of their assessments provide useful prototypes for alternatives to traditional assessment strategies.

As we note in Chapter 8, educators in Great Britain are in the forefront of thinking about and designing alternative assessments. Wynne Harlen's (1983) book, *Guides to Assessment in Education: Science*, describes a number of different approaches, among them observing in normal and special situations, summarizing achievements, and keeping different types of records. Pincus Tamir's work (undated), referred to earlier in this chapter, provides examples of paper-and-pencil assessment to use with older elementary children.

Another source of good alternative assessment tools is the Children's Learning in Science Project (CLIS) at the Centre for Studies in Science and Mathematics Education at the University of Leeds, England. Its useful publication is Paul Scott's (1987) *A Constructionist View of Learning and Teaching in Science*.

Key References

Harlen, W. (1983). *Guides to Assessment in Education: Science*. London: Macmillan Education.

Helm, H., and J. D. Novak. (1983). "Proceedings of the International Seminar in Science and Mathematics." Ithaca, N.Y.: Cornell University.

Raizen, S. A., J. B. Baron, A. B. Champagne, E. Haertel, I. V. S. Mullis, and J. Oakes. (1989). *Assessment in Elementary School Science Education*.

Andover, Mass.: The National Center for Improving Science Education, The NETWORK, Inc.

Raizen, S. A., and J. S. Kaser. (May 1989). "Assessing Science Learning in Elementary School: Why, What, How?" *Phi Delta Kappan* 70: 718-722.

Scott, P. (1987). *A Constructionist View of Learning and Teaching in Science.* Leeds, England: Centre for Studies in Science and Mathematics Education, the University of Leeds.

Tamir, P. (Undated). "Innovative Testing in Science." Unpublished manuscript. Jerusalem: School of Education and Israel Science Teaching Center, Hebrew University.

Yager, R. R. (October 1987). "Assess All Five Domains of Science." *The Science Teacher* 54: 33-37.

10.
Assess Programs as well as Students

Though important, assessing learning outcomes alone fails to yield the knowledge we need if we want to improve outcomes. Assessing other aspects of the science program—expectations for science learning for all students and for particular groups; program features, resources, and training available to teachers; and the level of access to science education for all students—will produce a more solid information base on which to make decisions about program needs and future directions.

WHAT WE KNOW

Consider the following scenario:

Scores on the district's achievement test battery have just come out, and one outcome worth noting is that the elementary schools have wide-ranging scores for science. In fact, scores within schools are even more spread apart than those between schools, yet some schools are clearly doing a better job with science than others. There are several possible next steps: (1) get the lower achieving teachers and schools to make a concerted effort to improve test scores by cramming, engaging in test preparation activities, and so on; (2) immediately schedule focused staff development efforts for the teachers and schools that are doing least well; and (3) identify and examine in a systematic way an array of program features that might influence the quality of science teaching, such as teacher expectations; resources and their availability; student, teacher, and administrator characteristics; and what is actually going on in classrooms.

Obviously, the last choice is the best. This exaggerated scenario makes the point that **what we know about science programs is often as important as, and sometimes more important than, what we know about science learning.**

If we know for a fact that student *learning* in science is rarely assessed—or rarely assessed well—then it should come as no surprise that examining the quality and characteristics of science programs is done even less frequently. Yet there are at least four important reasons to do so:

• Most educators, parents, and policy makers value the quality of resources, people, and activities that constitute children's learning experiences, and they have an interest in knowing more about them;

• Given the narrow range of learning outcomes that we currently measure in science, assessing program features would give educators a broader way of looking good, thereby lessening the obsession to perform well on tests;

• Although it is still unclear exactly what program characteristics lead to science learning, information about science programs can provide clues about why certain learning outcomes occur; and

• There is no way to determine why some learning outcomes might be particularly high or low unless there is information about *what was going on* in those classrooms or schools (Raizen et al. 1989).

The idea of program quality "indicators"—a word used more and more often by policy makers, especially at the state level—can help address the issue of program assessment because of its usefulness in identifying a program's features. These features can then be arrayed with learning outcomes to say what a program is like. When assessment systems include not only the narrowly defined learning outcomes of our current tests, but also indicators such as the resources available to teachers, their preparation and opportunity to improve their knowledge and skills, the expectations they hold for student learning, and what they actually *do* in their classrooms, a more rounded picture of "how we're doing in science" is achieved. In addition, indicators give many clues as to how to improve current programs.

Literature on science education and schooling suggests three areas as targets for program assessment:

• **Access to science knowledge:** the extent to which students have opportunities to learn various kinds of knowledge and skills. This includes hands-on activities and materials, time to learn, and knowledgeable teachers. Such an assessment involves disaggregating data to find out how these vary across population groups (e.g., girls and boys, minority groups, low achievers).

• **Press for science learning:** the schools' expectations of how well students will achieve in science and the degree to which teachers, students, and administrators act on these expectations. These include clear, informed, and solid goals for science learning, and expectations that *all* students will achieve the goals, including girls, minorities, and students with consistently lower achievement, as well as those who appear more able or focused on a career in science.

• **Teaching conditions:** the circumstances that enable and empower teachers and administrators to implement science programs that maximize access and create high expectations for student learning. These include opportunities (especially time) to create, select, plan for, and deliver good science curriculums and to do so collaboratively with other teachers; adequate programs and program materials; opportunities for professional development; and involvement in decisions about science programs (Raizen et al. 1989).

TAKING ACTION ON WHAT WE KNOW

What can we do to make science program assessment a routine practice at both the local and state level? Start by encouraging district and state evaluators to include a description of science program indicators in their assessment of science. This means helping them broaden what they measure beyond student learning outcomes (although, as we've argued earlier, these indicators in themselves need to be expanded from scores on tests assessing memorization of facts to include other ways of measuring additional outcomes). Assessments should also include program variables. Working with evaluators to establish a beginning set of indicators is important, since they can't measure everything (and will probably start by saying they can't measure anything else), and you'd want them to focus on things that most influence science learning. Also, consider working with them to develop a way of reporting indicators along with science learning outcomes that helps consumers of the information—policy makers, administrators, and the public—get a better handle on what's going on in the science program and thereby make more informed decisions about science education.

Assessing access to science knowledge is an important dimension of program assessment. Knowing about the following tangible characteristics of the science program can contribute to improvement goals:

- Instructional time devoted to science;
- Classroom assignment practices (ability-grouped or mixed instructional groups) and the curriculum associated with each ability group;
- Availability of high-quality instructional materials, laboratories, computers, and equipment, as measured against explicit standards that match curricular goals;
- Teachers' qualifications and experience in science;
- Use of science specialists or resource teachers;
- Availability of academic support programs (tutoring, afterschool remediation, etc.);
- Parents' involvement in science instruction or science activities;
- Opportunities for staff development in science; and
- Staff perceptions about the importance of science for all students.

There are many formats for program assessment, whether done by external evaluators or through self-assessment. Some groups have developed guidelines for schools or districts embarking on self-assessment. The National Science Teachers Association (1989), for example, has a plan for self-assessments that includes checklists for principals that cover an array of program characteristics. The state of Virginia has a resource guide that can be used both by external evaluators and local assessment teams (Virginia Department of Education 1986). The guide includes a data-collection and analysis plan; questionnaires for administrators, teachers, students, and parents; and a structured classroom observation instrument. School districts such as Weston, Massachusetts, have periodic self-assessments of curriculum areas that include external review teams and internal study of their programs.

Students can provide valuable feedback about what they like and do not like about a science program. Figure 10.1 is a survey used by the Minneapolis Public Schools.

Figure 10.1
Student Evaluation

1. Place an "X" under the column below that best describes how you liked the unit on seeds.

    Liked It   Liked It   It was O.K.   Disliked It   Disliked It
    a Lot   a Lot

    Why did you place an "X" where you did? _____

    _____ .

2. Describe what you liked best about learning about seeds._____

    _____ .

3. What part of learning about seeds did you not like? _____

    _____ .

4. Circle the number which best describes how you feel about the unit on seeds.

Easy	1	2	3	4	5	Hard
Boring	1	2	3	4	5	Exciting
Interesting	1	2	3	4	5	Uninteresting
Wow!!	1	2	3	4	5	Yuk!!

We also need to get a more in-depth picture of science program implementation. This can be accomplished by examining whether a science program's key features are being used by teachers and schools, and why or why not. Such an assessment was done in Jefferson County, Colorado, using the tools of the Concerns-Based Adoption Model (Loucks and Melle 1982). The district had revised its elementary science curriculum, using a comprehensive staff development plan and support system to help teachers implement the new program. As teachers in more than 80 elementary schools were helped to change their science teaching or, in some cases, to start teaching science, their Stages of Concern and Levels of Use of the new curriculum (Figure 10.2) were monitored. These concepts allowed district science leaders to learn how teachers' needs changed over time, what they were actually doing with the new program, and what kinds of help they needed.

Another way of determining the effect of the staff development program on teachers was to look specifically at how they implemented the various components of the curriculum. To do this, the district science leaders defined the program carefully, describing in 12 components what they expected to see happening in the school and classroom (Figure 10.3). Through interviews and observations, they assessed the extent of implementation for each teacher, as illustrated in Figure 10.4, a summary chart for a single school. (Each bullet [•] represents a single teacher.) Using these data along with those for Stages of Concern and Levels of Use, the science leaders could monitor the progress of their science program and examine how it had been implemented two and three years after the initial staff development. This program assessment allowed them to make sense of their achievement test scores, as well as to troubleshoot and determine where particular help and support were needed (Hall et al. 1980). The definition of 12 components was built into a handbook for principals that helped them observe and talk to teachers as they monitored use of the program. The handbook also includes strategies that can be used to increase teachers' extent of implementation (Jefferson County Schools 1979).

Figure 10.2

Stages of Concern: Typical Expressions of Concern About the Innovation

Stages of Concern		Expressions of Concern
6	Refocusing	I have some ideas about something that would work even better.
5	Collaboration	I am concerned about relating what I am doing with what other instructors are doing.
4	Consequence	How is my use affecting kids?
3	Management	I seem to be spending all my time in getting material ready.
2	Personal	How will using it affect me?
1	Informational	I would like to know more about it.
0	Awareness	I am not concerned about it (the innovation).

Levels of Use of the Innovation: Typical Behaviors

Leves of Use		Behavioral Indicators of Level
VI	Renewal	The user is seeking more effective alternatives to the established use of the innovation.
V	Integration	The user is making deliberate efforts to coordinate with others in using the innovation.
IVB	Refinement	The user is making changes to increase outcomes.
IVA	Routine	The user is making few or no changes and has an established pattern of use.
III	Mechanical	The user is making changes to better organize use of the innovation.

From Hord et al. 1987.

Figure 10.3
Components of the Revised Jefferson County
Elementary School Science Program (Grades 3–6)

1. The recommended percentage of teaching time during the day is devoted to science. An average of 15% of the student's day (10% for third grade) should be devoted to science.

2. Science is taught according to the district guide. During the school year the teacher teaches all units, all objectives of each unit, and 90% of the activities.

3. Students' learning is assessed according to the district science guide. According to a review of each unit, the teacher uses the guide assessments with students 85% of the time.

4. Basic skills, as differentiated by the continuum in each curriculum area, are being integrated into the science program. The basic skills keyed in the guide are being introduced or stressed in their subject area time allotment while they are being reinforced during science instruction.

5. The outdoors is used as a classroom when recommended. Whenever outdoor activities are recommended as part of a unit, they are always included.

6. All materials, equipment, and media are available. Appropriate commercial guides and the district guide are available for use. Enough materials are available for individual or small group usage. A storage system of logical sequence is established.

7. Principals have arranged for release of teachers for the total in-service training package and have allocated financial support to the program.

8. Long- and short-range planning is evident. The year's schedule is written out and being implemented by the teacher or the team. This schedule reflects attention to seasonal demands, sharing of materials, and maximum utilization of space and personnel. Before each unit is taught, overall planning for that unit takes place.

9. Class time in science is used effectively (time on task). At least 75% of the class time is devoted to exploration, pupil interaction, recording data, discussions and listening to each other. An efficient management system for distribution and clean-up of materials is evident.

10. Teacher-student interaction facilitates the program. Using the students' language, the teacher shares with students the objectives of the units. Discussion techniques include: neutral rewarding, wait time, questions above recall level, maximized use of student-student discussion, and data sharing.

11. The classroom environment and arrangement facilitates student-student interaction in small groups. Furniture and materials are arranged in order to facilitate small group interaction. Student behaviors include sharing of materials, listening to each other, working together toward a group goal, and interacting with each other (cooperative learning). Students are task-oriented most of the time.

12. The instruction in one classroom follows the stages of the learning cycle in science: exploration, concept formation, concept application.

Figure 10.4
Sample Building Summary Sheet

	Outside Intended Program 1	2	Getting a Good Start 3	Well on the Way 4	Best Practices Working 5
1. Time is devoted to science.	••• ••	•	••	•	••
2. Science is taught according to R.1 Guide.	••• •••	••• ••			
3. Assessment of pupil learning.	••• •••	••• ••			
4. Integration of basic skills.	•	••••• ••••	•		
5. The outdoor classroom is used as recommended.		••• ••	••• •	••	
6. Recommended materials, equipment, and media are available.			••• ••	••• •	••
7. Inservicing and financial arrangements have been made.		•	••• ••	••• ••	
8. Long- and short-range planning.		•••	••• •••	••	
9. Use of class time.	••	••	••••	••	•
10. Teacher-pupil interaction facilitates program.	•••	••••	••••		
11. Classroom environment facilitates program.		•••	•••	•••	••
12. Instruction is sequenced to facilitate the guided-inquiry learning approach.	••	•••• •	••••		

• = one teacher

School __Winter Elementary__   Teacher __All grade 3, 4, 5 6 teachers__

LOCAL ROLES

Things to do now:

1. **Work with district evaluators to develop a list of program characteristics** that can be examined along with student learning data for reporting on program quality and planning for improvement. Get input from teachers and administrators as well. Use these indicators in your next evaluation.

2. **Work with interested teachers to develop a component checklist** that defines the critical components of the science program, especially those that should be evident in the classroom. Conduct a study of the implementation of those components to help in planning for improvement. (See Loucks and Crandall 1982 to help develop component checklist.)

3. **Work with principals** to help them look for indicators of good science teaching. Encourage them to drop in on science classes and use the component checklist noted in Item 2 (above) to make informal observations.

Things to do for the future:

1. **Develop a method to represent the quality of the science program** to the community, school board, parents, and educators. The chosen vehicle needs to describe not only what the children are learning, but the features of the program as well. Describe program components in detail, and report change over time. Do not use to compare schools. An added benefit: Use for regular progress reports of the program.

2. **Pay special attention to equity issues** in designing, implementing, and reporting assessment information. Be sure to disaggregate data to get at the problem of great differences in access and expectations for different groups of students.

STATE ROLES

Things to do now:

Work with interested local science leaders to develop a set of indicators for quality science programs. Some might reflect ideas in this book, like curriculum organized around concepts, ongoing staff development, and a variety of approaches to student assessment.

Things to do for the future:

Educate state policy makers about the importance of indicators other than learning outcomes to assess the quality of science education. This can be done through presentation of program data along with outcome data and illustrations of how different program features accompany similar or different learning outcomes.

MODELS AND RESOURCES

A Local Model: The Jefferson County, Colorado, Public Schools' science department monitored the implementation of its revised elementary school science curriculum. The monitoring included examination over time of teachers' Stages of Concern, Levels of Use, and use of the program's 12 components. The program evaluation is described in Loucks and Melle (1982).

A Local Model: The Weston, Massachusetts, Public Schools have a unique program evaluation model that has the simultaneous goals of collecting good program data and enhancing communication and trust among the staff, scholars, school community, and the public. These groups are all represented on a review committee, which investigates issues generated by program staff, administrators, and parents. Using analysis of background materials and staff observations, interviews, and discussions, the committee drafts a report, which is used to build consensus among the staff about the contents of the final report.

A State Model: The Virginia State Department of Education's model for program assessment focuses on those elements believed to create a more effective learning environment. Either external evaluators or local school/community assessment teams can use its guide, *Science Education Program Assessment Model: A Resource Guide* (Virginia Department of Education 1986), which contains questionnaires for a variety of audiences and a structured classroom observation instrument. It also offers a set of model criteria that schools can compare their results to.

Key References

Hall, G. E., and associates. (1980). *Making Change Happen: A Case Study of School District Implementation.* Austin, Tex.: Research and Development Center for Teacher Education, the University of Texas.

Hord, S. M., W. L. Rutherford, L. Huling-Austin, and G. E. Hall. (1987). *Taking Charge of Change.* Alexandria, Va.: ASCD.

Jefferson County Schools. (1979). *A Principal's Handbook for Elementary Science.* Lakewood, Colo.: Jefferson County Schools.

Loucks, S. F., and D. P. Crandall. (1982). "The Practice Profile: An All-Purpose Tool for Program Communication, Staff Development, Evaluation, and Improvement." Andover, Mass.: The NETWORK, Inc.

Loucks, S. F., and M. Melle. (April 1982). "Evaluation of Staff Development: How Do You Know if It Took?" *Journal of Staff Development* 3, 1: 102-117.

Raizen, S. A., J. B. Baron, A. B. Champagne, E. Haertel, I. V. S. Mullis, and J. Oakes. (1989). *Assessment in Elementary School Science.* Andover, Mass.: The National Center for Improving Science Education, The NETWORK, Inc.

The National Science Teachers Association. (1989). *Guidelines for Self-Assessment, Elementary Programs.* Washington, D.C.: NSTA.

Virginia Department of Education. (1986). *Science Education Program Assessment Model: A Resource Guide.* Richmond, Va.: Virginia Department of Education.

11.
View Teacher Development as a Continuous Process

Teacher development is a long and complex task. It no more ends with preservice than learning stops at the end of one's formal education. To cultivate quality educators, teacher development needs to be an ongoing, well-planned effort in which a variety of organizations collaborate to develop and support the best teachers possible.

WHAT WE KNOW

Without a doubt, teachers are at the core of meeting the goals of education. The process of teacher development, therefore, deserves considerable attention. The challenge for the education community is to find and employ the best methods whereby a college student, with years of both exemplary and faulty learning experiences, can develop into a professional who creates ideal learning opportunities for children. To teach and assess the kind of science illustrated throughout this book requires a multifaceted repertoire of knowledge and skills that can be used to help children develop fundamental understandings of life, physical, space, and earth sciences, and scientific habits of mind. This charge, along with the continually changing nature of our scientific knowledge base, requires a new way of thinking about teacher development. Unfortunately, many elementary teachers have alarming gaps in what is needed to teach science. They do not know the content of science nor the methods for teaching science well. We therefore need new approaches of promoting the professional growth of teachers, especially in the science education arena.

From undergraduate liberal arts coursework through staff development for the most seasoned teachers, teacher learning needs to be continuous. With continuous learning as the norm, both prospective and current teachers can be helped to integrate and appropriately apply all of their learning experiences over time.

Here's a scenario that typifies most current teacher development practices:

As a prospective elementary school teacher, Adam attended an undergraduate school, taking liberal arts courses until beginning his professional education course sequence. He was not particularly interested in science, preferring language arts and reading. The two science courses required for graduation were not at all connected to any of his education courses. After student teaching, Adam was certified to teach because, after all, wasn't he now "a teacher"—able to take full responsibility for teaching an ever-broadening variety of increasingly complex content areas to a classroom brimming with children anxious to learn? After stumbling through his first year, learning on the job through trial and error, Adam found a wide range of staff development opportunities, including university coursework that would lead to another degree and a smorgasbord of district-sponsored inservice workshops. Adam routinely took courses that aligned with his particular areas of interest: language arts and reading. He rarely chose science-related inservice opportunities, and so he, like many of his colleagues, was hardly prepared to teach science. When a new science program was introduced, the one after-school inservice that was offered barely familiarized him with the new materials.

This scenario reflects the fragmented, discontinuous, and sporadic nature of current teacher development. It demonstrates why many elementary teachers are not well versed in science and science teaching. Through no fault of their own, they are not at all sure of the kinds of development they need to do their job well.

The implications of cases like this one are enormous. Consider, for example, the unfortunate circumstances that often surround unequipped new teachers, who struggle for the first year or two to handle a classroom only to abandon teaching altogether. Teachers who do persevere devote their efforts to the areas that interest them—and, most often, science is ignored. One-shot workshops that accompany new science texts or programs are hardly enough to do more than frustrate any teacher attempting to use an activity-based curriculum. Finally, and most important, students suffer. They receive minimal, if any, science instruction from people unprepared to make it the rich, intellectually stimulating, and exciting experience it can be.

The perspective on teacher development proposed in this book is built on a norm of continuous learning. This learning can begin during the undergraduate years. Preservice coursework needs to illustrate how content knowledge connects to pedagogical knowledge. When done well, undergraduate science courses use an experiential, constructivist approach to learning, helping students to *do* science and *think* about science as scientists do. They concentrate on in-depth development of scientific principles and the processes of science, rather than a multitude of facts.

An illustration of such a course is introductory geology at Carleton College in Northfield, Minnesota. Its goal is for students to act as scientists and perceive science as a way of behaving rather than as a body of knowledge. A typical textbook introduction to geology would begin with the earth and its place in the solar system and progress through matter and minerals, rocks, geologic cycle and geologic time, the evolution of the lithosphere, and geology and industry. Instead of using this textbook orientation, students are given a series of problems that require them to learn about various aspects of geology in order to solve them.

For example, the class might go to a river where several large gullies were apparently caused by erosion. Teams of students attempt to determine what is happening. Then the teams convene to discuss their observations, air their questions, and decide what further observations and information are needed. Back on campus, class meetings focus on gaining more information about the topic. Students discuss whose responsibility it is to stop erosion, how it could be stopped, and what scientific technology is available to stop it. In this way, knowledge is built, used, and applied to the same kind of problems for which students will need science in the future.

In addition to meaningful undergraduate coursework, noteworthy clinical experiences for teachers in training range from short, focused observations and one-on-one tutoring in class-rooms to planning and teaching small groups, well-supervised student teaching experiences, and internships. To help preservice teachers make meaning out of the acts of teaching and learning, these practical learning experiences must occur *before, during, and after* prospective teachers engage with information about child development and pedagogy. The settings for these experiences gradually move from the university campus to the school, with expert teachers in schools taking on increasing responsibility for modeling good teaching practices and overseeing the learning of prospective teachers.

The first two years of teaching deserve particular attention because new teachers still have much to learn, and most of them need help learning it. Being a new teacher is difficult, but there are various ways to successfully support them in their work. Less demanding teaching assignments and mentors who exemplify good teaching—especially constructivist science teaching—are two good examples. Besides serving as models, mentors provide support for the constant learning of new teachers as they become more and more comfortable in their classrooms.

The continuous learning perspective is invaluable for in-service teacher development as well. For new and veteran teachers alike, sporadic inservice workshops do not work. All staff development efforts need to be part of a developmentally sequenced plan that addresses new and improved teaching strategies and expands the base of content knowledge. In-depth training needs to be followed by coaching and other opportunities to engage with colleagues in learning about the changes teachers are making in their classrooms.

A commitment to continuous learning also means that teacher development strategies need to start from where teachers are. Whether in the early undergraduate years or after 20 years of teaching, teachers have different amounts of knowledge about science, learning, and teaching. Wherever staff development starts, we know from research on learning that true understanding and the ability to apply knowledge in adaptive and flexible ways require long-term study and multiple opportunities for application and practice. Well-planned, continuous teacher development is the only answer.

Finally, if teachers are to be good models for kids, they, too, need to be learners—preferably learners who demonstrate a love for learning and a hunger for knowledge. By exhibiting and fostering such behaviors, schools can become wholesome and exciting learning communities.

TAKING ACTION ON WHAT WE KNOW

To realize this vision of teacher development, organizations that prepare and support the ongoing development of teachers need to build appropriate structures and strategies. Here's how:

First, universities need to coordinate efforts between their science and education faculties. Science courses taken by prospective teachers need to incorporate the major organizing principles of science and technology and be taught in ways that model the processes of science. State science leaders can push for such a focus by asking that certification include courses taught in a way that models the process of science. It is essential that professors of education know that the goals of science education are to engage students in the process of science to facilitate concept development and to incorporate an understanding of the nature and processes of science and technology. Keeping this perspective, science education professors should model and reinforce pedagogy that helps preservice teachers reach these goals. Prospective teachers who have experienced good science teaching (i.e., who have learned science by doing science) have real experiences on which to base their learning of good science pedagogy.

Universities and schools, too, need to collaborate. Clinical experiences help prospective and new teachers make meaning of the ideas and skills they need to become expert teachers. But appropriate illustrations can be developed only if university faculty members and supervising teachers work together to develop settings in which what is being taught in college classes or student teaching seminars is illustrated in classrooms. At some universities, for example, at least half of the clinical professors' time is spent in schools, where they are available for regular consultation with student teachers. Professors can teach demonstration lessons for both new and experienced·teachers and work with faculty on planning and implementing a variety of school reforms. Collaborative structures, such as professional development schools, can provide a setting in which teachers have dual responsibilities for educating students and collaborating with university faculty in educating and mentoring new teachers (Holmes Group 1986, Schlechty et al. 1988).

Next, special beginning teacher programs should help new teachers gain the knowledge, skills, and confidence they need to take responsibility for a classroom full of kids. This calls for programs that are imbedded in the culture and reality of schools and provide (1) a mentor with the expertise to work closely with the new teacher, (2) time for both mentor and new teacher to observe each others' classrooms and discuss their observations, and (3) less difficult assignments for beginning teachers so they have ample opportunities to experiment and grow.

Staff development programs for teachers should include opportunities for them to begin where they are and get the input and support needed to make significant changes over time, based on district expectations for curriculum delivery and community expectations for education. Planning for this should have a long-term perspective and be based on teacher, program, and, ultimately, student needs. Appropriate approaches are discussed in the next section.

Finally, an organizational commitment is needed to the idea that the school is a learning community for the adults as well as the children connected to it. This creates expectations by teachers, administrators, and the community that teachers will continually add to their base of knowledge and skills. It allows teachers to return from workshops on constructivist learning and not be plagued by pressure to cover the textbook or have students succeed on fact-based tests. It also reinforces norms of experimentation and risk-taking, vital to both science learning and learning to be a better teacher.

LOCAL ROLES

Things to do now:

1. Form a principal/teacher advisory committee to compile and define staff needs and forward its requests to the district, state, local universities or colleges, and intermediate service agencies. In addition to requests, include some analysis of student learning opportunities and community desires for science learning. These staff development needs can be used for future planning and enable a broader development process to begin or continue.

2. Excite the superintendent, school board, all curriculum departments, and principals about science by updating them

on current science content with training that follows the recommended constructivist approach. Demonstrate how they can promote continuous learning by teachers so that science opportunities for children can broaden and deepen.

3. **Send out science news** about such things as eclipses, lift-offs, tracking of weather, and individual classroom science activities to make science an integral part of each day and help keep science excitement alive. This promotes the idea that teachers can and should be learners along with their pupils.

4. **Recognize teachers who add to their base of knowledge and skills** so that peers and the community are aware of their endeavors. Institute an annual Continuous Learning award for the person who exhibits the most love of learning and hunger for new knowledge.

Things to do for the future:

1. **Work with local universities and colleges to develop a model preservice program** that reflects the reforms recommended in this book. Encourage development of science courses such as those described for use with both undergraduates and inservice teachers who want to increase their knowledge of science content. Encourage education courses that are co-planned and co-taught by exemplary teachers and professors.

2. **Begin a mentor program** by identifying exemplary teachers, training them in adult learning and supervision strategies, and providing them with sufficient release time. Arrangements with local colleges and universities can be made to offset some of the costs if these mentors also serve as clinical professors or supervise student teachers.

3. **Replace sporadic inservices with long-term programs** that are carefully planned to develop new and improved teaching strategies; expand the base of content knowledge; and deal with local issues of implementation, program support, and integration of technology.

4. **Develop and offer varied opportunities** that stimulate, excite, and interest teachers. Institutes, sabbaticals, peer coaching, teacher-as-researcher programs, and supported study or inquiry are some examples.

STATE ROLES

Things to do now:

1. **Examine current state-supported preservice and inservice programs** to determine whether they support norms of continuous learning or whether they serve to separate science from pedagogy and preservice from inservice, and if they model one-shot learning opportunities or long-term, ongoing efforts. Encourage more collaboration within universities and between universities and schools by requiring it for grants, adjusting certification requirements, and so on. Encourage ongoing inservice opportunities by requiring extended training and follow-up support in grants, school improvement plans, and curriculum development and implementation efforts.

2. **Identify and recognize exemplary teachers.** Make their ongoing pursuit of knowledge a part of the selection criteria.

Things to do for the future:

1. **Design and implement a model for a well-planned, clearly defined staff development program** that affords opportunities for continuous learning for teachers in their efforts to become more proficient in teaching science. This program needs to be both in-depth and long-term. Support and reward districts that provide continuous staff development programs that have long-term impact. Encourage other districts to follow suit.

2. **Ask national bodies such as the National Science Foundation, the American Association for the Advancement of Science, and the National Science Teachers Association to hold institutes to update the knowledge and skills of local science leaders and teachers.** Include ideas such as the major concepts of science, science disciplines such as astronomy, and issues in science teaching such as teacher development and assessment of student learning. Offer extended institutes during the summer and shorter ones during the school year. Use teacher advisory groups to suggest the content, skills, and strategies they want.

3. **Initiate dialogue between colleges and districts** to find means of making continuous teacher development effective, convenient, and valued. Convene conferences in which collaborative efforts within and outside the state are featured and in which

participants can explore how they work. Include models of in-service teachers working as clinical faculty for universities. Also examine the idea of professional development schools, inviting several people who have designed and implemented them to come and describe how they work.

4. Initiate dialogue between university science and education faculties. Sponsor conferences that feature collaborative efforts, with opportunities for participants to explore how they work. Illustrate alternative organizational reward structures that allow such collaborative efforts to thrive.

MODELS AND RESOURCES

A University Model: The University of Northern Colorado has a model preservice program, Science and Mathematics for Elementary Preservice Teachers, which is supported by a five-year grant from the National Science Foundation and combines content and methods courses. Exemplary mentor teachers from the state's school districts work "on loan" with university faculty and bring the classroom into the college learning environment. The program employs a constructivist orientation, which is built around the expectation that teachers link instruction to students' developmental processes of shaping their own scientific notions. The project's science courses use such teaching strategies as inquiry and hands-on activities. These strategies are then evaluated and modified or expanded by students in methods courses.

A University Model: The University of New Hampshire offers a five-year teacher education program in which seasoned teachers play a major role in preservice instruction and taking the initiative in curriculum change efforts. The university also places students in collaborative action research projects that focus on improving the supervisory skills of principals and teachers working with preservice teachers.

A University Model: The University of Wyoming's Wyoming Center for Teaching and Learning coordinates most of the teacher development for the small and distant districts of the state. Working with preservice and seasoned teachers alike, the program integrates content and methods courses and helps teachers to employ an interdisciplinary approach to teaching science.

A Local Model: Carroll County, Maryland, schools have launched a comprehensive staff development effort to improve both the instructional strategies and science content expertise of their elementary teachers. The Carroll County program aims to help teachers implement a hands-on, process-oriented elementary science program and also addresses the issues of available classroom time for science instruction and methods for innovative assessment in the service of instruction.

Teachers were paid to attend a two-day summer workshop during which they experienced for themselves many of the activities they would be teaching in the classroom. They were grouped by grade level and trained by well-prepared peers on the first day. Day two of the workshop was conducted by an outside consultant who had ample classroom experience. After nine weeks, a one-day follow-up seminar helped teachers to resolve problems encountered in teaching the new program. Coaches from the University of Maryland's graduate school of education were used during the two-year implementation phase to give constructive feedback and help teachers with lesson plans and other instruction-related information. Forty-four exemplary teachers went on to participate in a graduate course in which they were trained in all grade levels of the elementary science program. These teachers then became a valued resource for other faculty.

Key References

Hall, G. E., guest ed. (January-February 1985). "Policies, Practices, Research: A Look at the Future." Special issue of the *Journal of Teacher Education* 36, 1: 2-68.

Holmes Group. (1986). *Tomorrow's Teachers: A Report of the Holmes Group.* Lansing, Mich.: Holmes Group.

Loucks-Horsley, S., M. O. Carlson, L. Brink, P. Horwitz, D. Marsh, H. Pratt, and K. Worth. (1989). *Developing and Supporting Teachers for Elementary School Science Education.* Andover, Mass.: The National Center for Improving Science Education, The NETWORK, Inc.

Loucks-Horsley, S., C. Harding, M. Arbuckle, C. Dubea, M. Williams, and L. Murray. (1987). *Continuing to Learn: A Guidebook for Teacher Development.* Andover, Mass.: The Regional Laboratory for Educational Improvement of the Northeast and Islands, and Oxford, Ohio: The National Staff Development Council.

Schlechty, P. D., D. W. Ingwerson, and T. I. Brooks. (1988). "Inventing Professional Development Schools." *Educational Leadership* 46, 3: 28-31.

12.
Choose Effective Approaches to Staff Development

Effective approaches to teacher development mirror what we know about learning; they are continuous, build on learners' current knowledge and skills, and include sufficient intensity and practice that new learnings can become part of teachers' ongoing practice.

WHAT WE KNOW

An analysis of research and experience in staff development (Loucks-Horsley et al. 1987) suggests that programs that effectively support teacher growth have the following characteristics:

• Content that is either based on research or has demonstrated its effectiveness in schools and classrooms;

• Opportunities for teachers to work together as they learn, plan to use, and implement their new knowledge and practices;

• Opportunities for teachers to participate in decisions about what they will learn, how they will learn, and how they will use what they learn;

• Norms that support experimentation and risk taking;

• Time for teachers to participate fully in the learning experience, to practice, to master new behaviors, and to incorporate new practices into their teaching routines;

• Integration of staff development into other initiatives of the school or district, with a connection between individual, school, and district goals;

• Leadership that provides direction and clear expectations, coupled with ongoing support for teachers to learn and to use what they learn;

• Appropriate and sufficient incentives and rewards; and

• Designs based on knowledge about learning and the process of change.

All of these characteristics are critical to the success of staff development. Yet the last is of particular interest here, since it is closely connected to our perspective of science learning. Although the implications of current cognitive research for adult learning strategies are not entirely clear, the constructivist perspective suggests some ways in which teacher learning mirrors the learning of students. It follows, then, that staff development should have much in common with what we described earlier as good science teaching. Among the characteristics they share are:

• Active learning techniques;

• Attention to what teachers already know (i.e., their current conceptions of science, of teaching, and of learning);

• Sufficient time to consider new ideas and "try them on" for fit; and

• Multiple opportunities to observe and then apply new knowledge in practice.

Thus, effective staff development can be an excellent model for good teaching.

TAKING ACTION ON WHAT WE KNOW

A constructivist-driven teacher development model suggests a certain course of action that is unlike traditional (primarily one-shot, workshop-oriented) staff development approaches.

Attention should be paid to prior teacher knowledge. Teachers at all levels of preparation come to teaching with their own experiences and observations of what works with children, what should be taught, and what instructional strategies work best. Preservice teachers, for example, may assume that engaging students with a good dose of creativity and enthusiasm is in and of itself enough fuel to ignite the learning fire. Experienced teachers may accept that engagement is essential to good learning but might also believe that reading about science qualifies as a stand-in for the exploration stage of the learning model. How can we begin to help teachers actively reconstruct their views about teaching and learning science if we don't attempt to pinpoint the prior knowledge teachers bring with them?

Concepts should be developed and introduced over sufficient periods of time. Just reading or hearing about new concepts is rarely enough to advance authentic learning. Teachers need to participate in multiple, interactive, collaborative experiences. For example, rather than learn about the topic of pond life via a one-time, facts-to-be-learned presentation, teachers can work in small groups to share what they know and then, visiting an actual pond, work together to reconstruct their views. This type of learning will allow them to develop their understanding of such concepts as diversity and systems over time.

Theory should be tied to experience by using learning activities that make abstract concepts personal. Such experiences are the catalysts that help teachers learn. Follow this with activities that give teachers time to reflect on their experiences. Then introduce new information that prompts teachers to focus on the formation of abstract concepts and generalizations. To continue with our pond life example, teachers can design aquariums for their classrooms so they (and their students) can observe and answer questions that relate to pond life. They can also divide readings, relate the readings to what they observe, and share their findings with each other. Concept development continues in this phase as teachers digest new information. The instructor slowly adds fuel as discussions turn to formal theories such as food webs, interdependency of pond organisms, ecosystem factors that enable pond life, and so on. Learners can personally experience concepts when the methods of experiential engagement and exploration, along with theory conceptualization and the pedagogical techniques of small working groups, are employed. Here theory ties closely to experience.

In the final step, teachers should have opportunities to try out developing concepts by making multiple applications in their classrooms. Teachers need the chance to experiment with new concepts and techniques with their students. At meetings held after their trials, teachers can compare successes and strategies about back-to-the-drawing-board activities.

As a follow-up, a long-term plan should be instituted for supporting novices. Give teachers a voice in how this process will work. They may elect to form support or check-in groups, designate those who are most expert as mentors, or continue to refine applications with their original work group.

This model suggests that we view the teacher development process, from beginning coursework through inservice opportunities, from a constructivist perspective that encourages teachers to explore, experience, and incorporate new strategies. Teachers need to decide when, how, and under what conditions these new strategies should be used. This approach prepares teachers to deal with increasing classroom diversity and a multitude of daily decisions. It also allows them to construct an evolving instructional theory in the classroom, regardless of which science curriculum they use.

Learning More About Science

In Chapter 11, we note that most of today's elementary school teachers have limited knowledge of science. They were not required to take much science as undergraduates, and the courses they did take were not taught in a way that allowed them to develop concepts they would need to teach. In addition, few elementary teachers consider science their favorite subject, and so, when given the choice of a potpourri of inservice offerings, they don't choose to learn more about science. This may also be because the offerings don't promise to help them much in the long run.

What would a good science offering—whether at the preservice or inservice level—look like? Such a course, institute, or workshop would:

• **Be taught in a way that reflects constructivist learning**. This means learners would do science by pursuing real questions about the natural world and mixing investigative methods with knowledge about the important facts and concepts of science as a discipline. Depth of content rather than breadth of coverage would lead to desirable concept formation instead of rote memorization of science trivia.

• **Use an interdisciplinary approach** so that a geology course, for example, would incorporate biology, chemistry, mathematics, and physics. Teachers will then see the interrelationships that occur naturally in the real world and are not separated into disciplines.

• **Include historical and philosophical assumptions and contexts**. Some early philosophical theories can help us understand present-day laws and ideologies, including a few of the misconceptions students (and teachers) bring to class. For instance, Aristotle believed that forced motion is maintained by force. Buriden's impetus theory developed from Aristotle's notion and maintains that the impetus is an internal source of force that maintains the motion. These views contrast with Newton's laws, which suggest that an object in motion tends to stay in motion unless a force acts upon it.

• **Help teachers relate science content to technological and societal issues**, thereby connecting science to the real world and how we live in it. A unit on waste pollution, for example, might consider an alternative to the present use of styrofoam materials.

• **Use instructional strategies** like cooperative learning, wait time, discussion techniques, inquiry, problem solving, and assessment, so that teachers witness for themselves how these methods serve as important vehicles for science learning.

• **Introduce problem solving** as an active means for learning the important facts and concepts of science.

• **Require collaboration among faculty from several disciplines or fields**. Whatever course is being taught would benefit from a number of perspectives, especially when instructors make it a point to connect content of different disciplines. This can be done using a life science/physical science team or a science/pedagogy team.

As an example, the introductory geology course at Carleton College of Northfield, Minnesota—discussed in Chapter 11—could be used as the basis of a teacher workshop in geology that incorporates the model described herein at either the preservice or inservice level:

It might begin the same way, with groups of participants embarking on a field trip to a river where gullies were apparently formed by erosion. Participants would work to solve the problem of identifying and explaining what is happening. They would observe, wonder, ask questions of each other, and discuss what additional information is needed. This phase represents the invitation and exploration stages of learning, and the instructor uses the activity as an informal assessment of previous learnings and views about geology, erosion, the action of rivers, and so on.

Back at the workshop, with the instructor's help and resource books, teachers gain additional information on the topic. The instructor uses the questions raised as a guide to decide if the class needs to return to the area, visit a different one, conduct an in-class water erosion activity, or view a media presentation. Interactions between participants and the instructor, with materials, and among participants are all helpful for information gathering. The process helps participants to further define concepts and begin to form explanations. At this point, it's appropriate to introduce the history of the area in terms of both geological and human impact. The instructor might opt to bring in a social science instructor, a senior citizen, or a local businessperson who could discuss the impact of the geological development. Connections between what was, what happened and why, and what might be needed can be introduced with the best pedagogical strategies. Wait time during questioning and small- group discussions can be important here.

The instructor uses a culminating activity to assess the effectiveness of the instruction, focusing on the level of new knowledge gained, problem-solving abilities acquired, and participants' concept formation. A team debate on how the community might work together to stop erosion, and how new technologies might help, would be an excellent vehicle for such an assessment.

This course models for teachers how children need to be learning in their classrooms. It weaves together important science knowledge, skills, and attitudes, and uses different approaches to assessment. Employing a variety of instructional strategies helps make learning science an enjoyable—even exciting—experience for students and teachers alike.

Learning More About Learning

What teacher development approach would foster a rich understanding of how children learn? Such a course, institute, or workshop would:

• **Extend over a long period of time**, encouraging developing teachers to incorporate into their knowledge bases an expanding picture of how children develop and learn. They are continually involved in constructing a more elaborate understanding of children, how they most effectively learn science, and, subsequently, what instructional strategies are most appropriate to use and how and when they could be used best.

• **Provide teachers with knowledge about the complete range of theories and research on children's learning**, including developmental findings from research on social learning, behaviorism, and more recent work in cognitive learning theory. Constructivism has had and will continue to have an important impact on elementary school science and how it is taught. Teachers need to understand the theory behind constructivism and see the implications it has for curriculum, instruction, and assessment.

• **Be simultaneously rich in theory and research and experientially based.** Coursework in how children learn must allow preservice teachers to work directly with children during science learning to see how to apply the theoretical principles they are learning. Constructivism provides a model of how such a course might be framed. Early in the course, for example, participants might visit classrooms to observe how children learn science. They share observations and discuss in teams which of the instructional strategies and techniques worked and which did not, as well as why and how they worked. At this point teachers are ready to learn some new information, perhaps something about developmental learning theory, that will enhance their developing concept of how children learn.

• **Not confine learning about learning to courses devoted solely to theories of learning.** For instance, in some buildings teachers may form collegial teams to share their insights into how children learn science and to invite expert guests to share with them aspects of how children learn. Teachers could examine curriculum materials and see how the instructional format reflects one or more learning theories. The format for the Elementary Science Study units is quite different from the materials for Science: A Process Approach. A major determinate of those differences lies in the different theories of learning that the curriculum developers used to structure activities.

Schools and districts can choose among several approaches for teacher development that can incorporate these characteristics (see Sparks and Loucks-Horsley 1989 for detailed discussion):

• **Training with coaching.** Most frequently equated with staff development, this approach can result in demonstrable changes in teacher behavior and, subsequently, in the behaviors of children. The model includes development of the theory and rationale behind the new behaviors to be learned, demonstration or modeling, practice in training settings, and guided practice or peer coaching in the classroom with supportive feedback from a colleague. The process of peer coaching is particularly important in helping teachers change their teaching practices, in providing them with opportunities to discuss their changing ideas about teaching, and in giving them the psychological support they need to persist in learning (Joyce and Showers 1988).

• **Observation and assessment.** This approach involves careful observation of teaching with attention to certain behaviors and an open discussion of the results. The model is labeled in various ways, primarily as forms of supervision and coaching. Teachers agree on a focus for the observations, with the observer recording behaviors as they occur. A conference follows, in which the observations are discussed, strengths and weaknesses assessed, and goals set for the future. Both the observed teacher and the observer can gain insight into effective pedagogy and how to incorporate it into daily teaching practice.

• **Inquiry.** This approach incorporates such practices as action research and reflective inquiry. Teachers, alone or collaboratively, decide what problem or situation they are interested in examining, gather and analyze data, and interpret the results in light of changes they might make in their classrooms or in school practice.

• **Individually guided staff development.** In this approach, teachers, individually or in collegial teams, identify their interests and concerns; establish a goal; and seek input by way of coursework, workshops, library research, field trips, and other forms of self-study to reach the goal.

These approaches to staff development can complement, and in some cases replace, the traditional inservice workshop. When well designed, they can help teachers increase their knowledge of science, learning, and teaching in ways that they can apply directly to classroom teaching.

LOCAL ROLES

Things to do now:

1. **Examine current staff development offerings** to determine whether they have the characteristics described in this chapter. Consider adding components to increase learning.

2. Consider alternative approaches to inservice workshops that either replace or complement the workshops. Peer coaching, a teacher-as-researcher program, individually guided staff development—all can extend and reinforce important learnings.

3. Make better use of internal expertise. Identify exemplary science teachers to test new programs and become trainers for their peers. Have high school science teachers teach science content to elementary teachers. Prepare teachers to be good staff developers by helping them use a constructivist perspective to design and deliver their instruction.

Things to do for the future:

1. Work with local universities to change the nature of their science and education coursework. Develop collaborative programs using exemplary science teachers, school settings, and different approaches to teacher preparation.

2. Develop closer links with the community to bring teachers real-world experiences from which to learn. Contact local businesses and industries, and work with science professionals to plan inservice offerings and placement opportunities.

STATE ROLES

Things to do now:

1. Promote good staff development by making school and district inservice coordinators and science leaders aware of the characteristics of good staff development programs and alternatives to inservice workshops. Give examples of how to change current practice.

2. Model good staff development practices in state-sponsored events, institutes, and teacher enhancement programs. Incorporate alternative approaches such as coaching and teacher inquiry.

Things to do for the future:

1. Target grant monies to schools and districts that incorporate characteristics of good staff development into their program plans.

2. **Identify exemplary staff development programs and practices, and put them "on the road.**170 Maintain an up-to-date listing of staff development offerings in districts in the state, and develop networks for sharing expertise.

3. **Work with universities to improve the quality of course teaching.** Provide opportunities to learn about exemplary practices, share expertise, and design alternative strategies.

4. **Begin a statewide Alliance for Science Education within your state.** Contact university scientists, science educators, and professional scientists employed by businesses about building a program that improves learning opportunities for teachers.

MODELS AND RESOURCES

An Association: The Association for Constructivist Teaching is a professional educational organization that identifies and disseminates effective constructivist practices for student and teacher development. The Association provides its members with resources, an annual conference, professional networks, and a quarterly newsletter.

A Book: In *Enquiring Teachers, Enquiring Learners: A Constructivist Approach to Teaching*, Catherine T. Fosnot (1989) shares an innovative model of teacher education in which, rather than being spoon fed, the learner is engaged in questioning, hypothesizing, investigating, imagining, and debating instructional strategies. Fosnot includes detailed "how to" course descriptions on topics such as activities that engage teachers as learners.

A Teacher Education Model: The teacher education program at Michigan State University is designed to prepare teachers who are skilled in teaching for conceptual change. Using a course of study that promotes conceptual change in the prospective teachers themselves, the program is based on recent cognitive research, especially research currently under way at Michigan State.

A Teacher Education Model: Science methods courses at Purdue University use the Generative Learning Model to help prospective teachers construct knowledge about science teaching. (Use of the four-stage teaching model is described in Kyle et al. 1989.)

Key References

Brooks, M. G., and J. G. Brooks. (Fall 1987). "Becoming a Teacher for Thinking: Constructivism, Change, and Consequence." *Journal of Staff Development* 8, 3: 16-20.

Caldwell, S., ed. (1989). *Staff Development: A Handbook of Effective Practices.* Oxford, Ohio: The National Staff Development Council.

Fosnot, C. T. (1989). *Enquiring Teachers, Enquiring Learners: A Constructivist Approach to Teaching.* Wolfeboro, N.H.: Teachers College Press.

Joyce, B., and B. Showers. (1988). *Staff Development and Student Achievement.* New York: Longman.

Kyle, W. C., Jr., S. Abell, and J. A. Shymansky. (Spring 1989). "Enhancing Prospective Teachers' Conceptions of Teaching and Science." *Journal of Science Teacher Education* 1, 1: 10-13.

Loucks-Horsley, S., M. Carlson, L. Brink, P. Horwitz, D. Marsh, H. Pratt, and K. Worth. (1989). *Developing and Supporting Teachers for Elementary School Science Education.* Andover, Mass.: The National Center for Improving Science Education, The NETWORK, Inc.

Loucks-Horsley, S., C. Harding, M. Arbuckle, C. Dubea, M. Williams, and L. Murray. (1987). *Continuing to Learn: A Guidebook for Teacher Development.* Andover, Mass.: The Regional Laboratory for Educational Improvement of the Northeast and Islands, and Oxford, Ohio: The National Staff Development Council.

Sparks, D., and S. Loucks-Horsley. (Fall 1989). "Models of Staff Development." *Journal of Staff Development* 10, 4: 40-59.

13.
Provide Teachers with Adequate Support to Implement Good Science Programs

Science programs won't move very far off the launch pad if encouragement and the tools of the trade are missing. The best science teaching occurs when teachers have the organizational, psychological, and material support needed to do their jobs well.

WHAT WE KNOW

In Chapters 11 and 12 we explore the types of teacher development activities that prepare teachers to teach science well. Yet even well-prepared teachers need additional supports in the areas of organizational structure, materials management, and psychological nourishment that sustain the belief that science is indeed valuable and they can do a good job teaching it. Before we examine these supports, let's look at the **current conditions that inhibit elementary teachers from teaching science well** (Weiss 1987). They include:

• The uncertainty with which most teachers approach teaching science;

• The emphasis in elementary schools on language development and math, and the lack of attention given to science;

• The lack of a well-defined elementary science program with all the curriculum and support materials needed for the instruction of good science lessons;

• The lack of a well-planned staff development program geared to the improvement of science teaching; and

• Teachers' feelings of not being appreciated, of being isolated, and of being out of control regarding decisions about how best to teach the children for whom they are responsible.

Many of these issues can be addressed by taking a critical look at the organizational structures and supports (or lack thereof) in schools. It's critical that these systems work for teachers because, **of all the factors involved in the teaching of science, the most important is the classroom teacher.** Teachers need to be valued in demonstrable ways. In the business world, for instance, it is known that valued workers are more productive. This is no different for teachers. They are critical to their students' success.

There is little definitive research on how organizational structures influence the quality of science teaching. But we do have documentation on educational quality, teacher professionalism, policy implementation, effective schools, and educational change—all of which are directly related to the issue of teacher competency. This research suggests that high-quality education occurs in environments in which teachers are supported in five important ways:

1. Clear purposes and outcomes. Expectations for program goals and outcomes help teachers stay on course and move together in a productive direction. Standards of excellence for curriculum, instruction, and assessment should all be articulated. Who should establish program goals and outcomes? Though several national frameworks exist (AAAS's Project 2061 and the National Center's work are two examples), states may provide the most appropriate direction given their control over so many of the variables that can enhance or detract from good science teaching. In states with a history of local control, or that do not possess a goal-setting capacity, districts can set purposes and outcomes for science learning.

2. Resources and their allocation. What happens in the elementary classroom is directly influenced by available resources, time, and staffing. To adequately prepare students to become scientifically literate, students need to spend between 120 (K-3) and 300 (4-6) minutes per week on science and technology education. Right now, students are spending only 100 minutes or less per week learning science. We therefore need to make science a priority by allocating more time for science education. And to make that time worthwhile, there needs to be additional attention to staff development, adequate materials and equipment, and adequate facilities; these factors contribute to good science teaching, and all will require more resources.

3. A rich conception of staff development. Our new vision of exemplary science education requires a comprehensive teacher development strategy that continually confronts a complex range of issues linked to the district's overall goals and priorities (Odden and Marsh 1988). Disconnected staff development offerings will need to be replaced with an orchestrated set of courses that tie together state, district, and local frameworks for curriculum, instruction, and assessment. Involving groups of teachers or, better yet, all teachers within a school, in the same training, constitutes a critical mass that can help changes get implemented and then maintained. State and district science leaders as well as principals and other administrators can benefit from leadership development efforts. They can learn the delicate balance between alternately doling out support and applying appropriate pressure to struggling staff members.

4. Organizational norms that support constructivist learning. The constructivist science that we propose in this book requires that the classroom become a place for experimentation, risk taking, questioning, and collaborative problem solving. This can evoke more than a small amount of anxiety for many teachers. But if schools encourage and expect teachers to engage in these behaviors, the chance that they will develop their science teaching skills becomes much greater.

5. Involvement in decision making. Teachers who are knowledgeable and skilled in the teaching of constructivist science are in the best position to decide what should be taught and when. Clearly, they know their students better than anyone, and they need autonomy to make critical decisions, adjusting instruction to students' developmental needs, current understandings, and interests. We know from research that involvement in decision making can heighten teachers' ownership in their programs (Lightfoot 1983) and even reduce absenteeism and teacher turnover (Darling-Hammond 1986).

This is not to suggest that individual teachers should have total autonomy over their students' science education. For one thing, most elementary teachers are *not* skilled in teaching constructivist science, nor are they committed to doing so. Typically, elementary teachers are better prepared in and favor the areas of language arts and reading. Further, teachers have neither the time nor the expertise (nor, oftentimes, the interest) in determining scope and sequence for their grade level, for their elementary schools, or for their district's K-12 science education program. Nor are they up to date on what makes good science curriculum and instruction and what materials and programs are available to support them.

That said, teachers can and should help make decisions about science programs and curriculum, especially decisions that directly affect their students. Involvement of teachers on committees and task forces is critical if these decisions are to result in doable programs. At the school and grade or teaching team level, teachers can make program implementation decisions, including how and when to introduce new curriculums, how best to structure and deliver staff development, who should be teaching what, how teachers can support each other's teaching, and what special adaptations are needed for their students. Such decision-making prerogatives not only build ownership in teachers, but also the commitment to develop their own knowledge and skills to improve their teaching.

TAKING ACTION ON WHAT WE KNOW

Organizational Support

District and building administrators can demonstrate organizational support for teachers by sending a clear message that the elementary science program is a priority and by articulating clear expectations, purposes, and outcomes for the program. There is general consensus that people are more productive in their work environments when they know the what, how, and why of the structure, practices, and parameters within which they operate. For example, teachers can be more productive if they know which organizing principles the curriculum is built on and what instructional model supports the chosen principles. The development of clear purposes and outcomes helps teachers gain a sharp focus on the common agenda.

Organizational support should also include **actions by principals and others responsible for science education that help elementary teachers in their efforts to teach good science.** For instance, administrators can:

• Stop a teacher in the hall and ask how his science unit is progressing, what kinds of questions the students are asking, or what type of investigations they are developing;

• Provide teachers with information about science opportunities, such as new programs, conferences, meetings, and inservice workshops, and make funds or substitutes available so teachers can participate in pairs or teams;

• Create opportunities for teachers to share what they learn through both outside activities and their own experimentation;

• Take over a class for teachers so that they can coach their peers, team teach, or observe exemplary science teaching;

• Advocate science education by keeping the media aware of exciting things that are happening in the classrooms;

• Provide teachers with a petty cash fund for science activities;

• Organize a science field trip for teachers on a Saturday, and make it fun and exciting;

• Start some faculty meetings with a short, engaging science activity;

• Arrange for local scientists or science teachers to make presentations to classes;

• Arrange to have student presentations of science activities featured at a P.T.A. meeting;

• Support teachers in extracurricular science activity projects such as Invent America!, science olympiads, or energy fairs;

• Make it clear that science teaching (and the mess that goes with it) takes precedence over the needs of the custodians; and

• Nominate leading teachers for the new Elementary School Presidential Awards in science.

Figure 13.1
Roles for Principals

(Adapted from Mechling and Oliver 1983)

Here are some important roles for principals:

- *The principal as science leader:* Principals demonstrate leadership in and positive attitudes toward science education and communicate their interest in science to teachers and others.

- *The principal as curriculum analyst:* Principals investigate their own science programs in terms of goals, teaching strategies, typical learning experiences, evaluation procedures, and so on.

- *The principal as a force in the selection or development of a new science curriculum:* Principals provide leadership in curriculum choice or development. As a driving force and catalyst, they push to get the process going and keep it on track.

- *The principal as provider of the wherewithal:* Principals seek funds to purchase science supplies and equipment, cover costs of staff development, and ensure that supplies are readily available for teacher use.

- *The principal as provider of inservice instruction:* Principals take the lead in providing inservice experiences in science for their teachers.

- *The principal as a monitor of progress in science programs:* Principals give their science programs periodic checkups to determine their validity and continuing effectiveness.

- *The principal as troubleshooter:* Principals deal effectively with problems that arise in the science curriculum, like teachers having difficulty fitting science into their crowded day, over-reliance on reading as a method of teaching science, classroom noise, and inconvenient schedules or access to materials or equipment.

Administrators can help teachers become competent decision makers by creating opportunities and structures in which they can become involved in decisions about implementing curriculum, instruction, and teacher development. For example, teachers should be given a chance to collaborate on their own professional development. They should be provided opportunities to share expertise, coach their peers, solve problems, and pursue their own improvement. Time and settings can be arranged for them to share their knowledge about how students learn, what teaching approaches work in different areas of science and technology education, and what topics and themes might be appropriate vehicles for teaching the major concepts, skills, and attitudes that we recommended earlier in this book. A climate that communicates that everyone has something to learn and that everyone can benefit from others' experience is essential.

Funds for teacher release time can be (re)allocated for staff development by:

- Establishing more personal professional days;
- Arranging for roving substitute teachers to release teachers for an hour of peer observation, team planning, and so on;
- Specifying early release days on a regular basis;
- Hiring teachers with expertise on an extended contract for work in the summer with district personnel and principals; and
- Combining several classes to release teachers.

Teachers who demonstrate excellence in teaching constructivist science should serve as workshop planners and leaders and demonstrate classroom teaching. They should plan for teacher development by working with district personnel, board members, principals, peers, and the community. Administrators can showcase lead teachers by recommending them to the state for recognition, using them as key committee members, and publicly recognizing their expertise.

Teachers should be systematically rewarded for good science teaching and an ongoing commitment to their own learning. Both external and intrinsic rewards are appropriate motivators for teachers to continue their professional development. Effective staff development systems provide a variety of options for rewards: additional pay and opportunities to train others, to travel, and to work collaboratively. Intrinsic rewards are probably even more powerful. The opportunities we have listed above should spur teachers to share ideas; reach out for innovative, effective teaching practices; and increase the knowledge of their craft. It's highly rewarding and motivating when a teacher masters a new teaching strategy and then goes on to become a teacher of teachers. Such personal success reaffirms the belief that one can make a difference in the lives of children as well as adults.

Psychological Support

Teachers feel supported in environments that champion openness and have norms that encourage them to be experimenters, risk takers, and team players. Doing science is a way of knowing about the world around us. In the elementary grades, good science teaching encourages students to wonder, to explore, and to develop conceptions of how the world works. To teach science effectively, teachers need the license to investigate, try new ways of doing things, and work with others to share and solve problems. Strategies that help teachers themselves become science students will effectively support science education.

Psychological support is also demonstrated when teachers feel that their concerns and needs are being taken care of. In Chapter 10, we describe seven stages of concern that can be used to monitor changes in how teachers feel about their science programs. These stages are also useful to pinpoint teachers' needs and questions so they can be responded to. For example, when teachers have management concerns, they can use help with making better use of time, getting and organizing materials, and managing classroom activities. Since it's possible to predict how concerns will change over time, one can design an implementation effort that addresses teachers' needs as they emerge through materials, workshops, in-class assistance, and so on. It's usually a relief to teachers when administrators assure them that change takes time and perfect performance is not expected overnight. Being sympathetic to individual concerns and having the right kind of help available when it's needed are what we mean by psychological support.

Material Support

To teach science well and avoid frustration, teachers need appropriate and easily accessible resources. Needed support includes providing materials for teaching, creating an environment that sustains a constructivist science program, allowing time to prepare for teaching good science, and considering options for teacher assistance, like having a science resource teacher available. Consider implementing one or more of the following ideas:

1. **A resource list,** perhaps taken from the National Science Resources Center's (1989) *Science for Children: Resources for Teachers,* of curriculum and material vendors, publishers, and distributors, complete with addresses, phone numbers, and prices. The resources selected should reflect program goals. The list must be

easily accessible (e.g., included in curriculum guides or the like) and be updated yearly.

2. An in-house news vehicle such as a newsletter or electronic mail. This can serve several important functions: to announce workshops and new resources; to organize for materials management; to create opportunities for teachers and others to share ideas; and to alert people to relevant current events, problems, and so on.

3. An organizing system for media resources (e.g., films, videos, computer software) that are used in the science program. A list of all items used by grade level in the program is essential. Additionally, a "prepare ahead of time" list can help with teacher preparation and organization. The title, order number, and location (central distribution media center, school media center, individual kits) all need to be clear and accurate. A budget that provides for adequate copies of any one title ensures that use will occur at the best learning point for students instead of whenever the title is available.

4. A system of storage and retrieval for all printed materials that includes information on when and how to use them and where to get supplementary resources if they are not provided. One person in charge (teacher, media specialist, principal, district person) prepares and monitors an inventory that is ready, appropriate, and available for use. Laissez-faire or honor system approaches often lead to disappearing materials and a greater drain of funds.

5. A system for purchasing, packaging, storing, and replenishing hands-on science materials. Considerations for such a system include:

• *Reusable materials* that can be recycled for a number of years if not broken or lost. Kits need good packaging if they are going to last. When purchasing a program, examine its packaging; do not accept inadequate materials. If packaging your own kits, buy the best boxes possible.

• *Storage areas* in each building or central to the district. These need to be sufficient to prevent teachers from getting damaged test tubes, shattered light sources, and crushed materials boxes.

• *A retrieval/inventory system* handled by one individual. The program will not be taught if materials are not complete, easy to assemble and get, or damaged. Inventory lists, including the number of each item per classroom, are needed on all kits at the beginning of each unit in the curriculum guide.

- *Consumable materials* need to:
  — be listed by unit *and* by all units for the year in curriculum guides;
  — have local sources identified;
  — be budgeted for each year, with yearly totals given to the principal for budget planning; and
  — have a replenishment system in which teachers know who buys, with what money, on what person's request, with how much lead time, and so on.

Each district and school is responsible for deciding how to best manage science equipment and materials. A materials support system helps make science instruction easier. When organized at the school level, the librarian might house and manage the materials. Or one teacher or a school secretary might assume the responsibility for ordering, storing, and disseminating materials, when provided the time to do so.

A districtwide system for materials management is most cost-effective. This may involve a central science kit system or science center where supplies of commercial kits or locally developed materials and other items are stored and resupplied. This allows for bulk purchasing and sharing of equipment and supplies. Sharing materials will mean a wider range of units available for students. Another advantage of establishing a science center is that it serves as a tangible focal point of the elementary science program for teachers, administrators, and the community, thereby promoting science education. Materials such as posters available from the U.S. Forest Service, to be used by a large number of teachers, would have a home in the science center. Through such a centralized system, districts can maximize working with private industry to develop materials and kits for units like mining and minerals. A well-organized central program in which staff routinely update materials and sign out materials systematically can go far to optimize the use of resources for science teaching. (For examples of such systems, see the Models and Resources section.)

ONE PLAN OF ACTION

There are many possible ways to begin to design or overhaul an elementary school science program. Under Local Roles and

State Roles, we describe many starting points for and components of long-term change. Here, however, is one quick start-up strategy for a district that wants to start tomorrow to make a difference in science learning. This strategy includes:

1. **A shared leadership team of selected teachers and administrators** who assess the current state of science teaching and resources, select a science program, oversee training and support for teachers, monitor progress, and communicate regularly both inside the system and with the community.

2. **An existing, exemplary science program** selected from among those recognized by NSTA in its Focus on Excellence Program, the National Diffusion Network, or those described in the National Science Resources Center's (1989) *Science for Children: Resources for Teachers* (see Models and Resources section for more information), and adapted for use with the particular student population and resource base.

3. **A set of pilot teachers** who, with help from the program's developer, spend a year mastering the program and being prepared as a *training and support cadre* for full implementation.

4. **A two-year training sequence for all**, with the first year having up to three days of release-time workshops in which teachers learn how to teach the units, and with the second year having up to three days devoted to improving teachers' understanding and skills in constructivist teaching, cooperative learning, and approaches to assessment.

5. **A support structure** that provides teachers with all the materials they need for teaching and makes individual help and coaching available to them on a regular basis.

6. **A program of awareness and training for people other than teachers** (such as principals, library and media specialists, and resource teachers) to orient them to the new program, how it relates to other programs, and the support roles they need to play.

Others may want to begin their efforts to improve support for science teaching in different ways. Below are some roles that local and state educators can use to begin on the road to long-term change.

LOCAL ROLES

1. **Carefully plan and develop an elementary science curriculum.** Specify what is to be taught, the strategies to be used,

and the time frame for teaching the curriculum. Include on the development committee teachers who, although they may not be expert science teachers, recognize the importance of teaching science well. Also include principals and district administrators. Consider exemplary district programs, programs from the National Diffusion Network, and curriculum currently under development for adoption or adaptation. Review materials, make visits, and try out sample units to help make a decision.

2. Develop policies and procedures, and articulate them to teachers. Clearly defined procedures help to ensure that staff members will be treated fairly and equally. Trust is fostered when teachers know what to expect and what is expected of them.

3. Plan for and implement a materials management system. Design a system appropriate to the schools' and district's resources, science curriculum, and staff capabilities.

4. Recognize the principal's role in supporting an elementary science program. Provide principals with special training in that role, including enough about the curriculum and instructional strategies for them to recognize it in classrooms and help teachers find help if they need it. Encourage principals to allow for release time through schedule manipulations and to set a climate that includes the expectation, encouragement, and praise for teachers to teach science well. Principals can encourage staff members to share their knowledge and experience by inviting them to form collegial teams, recommending that they take lead roles on district committees, and involving them in decisions about implementing the science curriculum.

5. Promote collaboration as a means of personal support for teachers. Provide opportunities for teachers to work together as they try new activities and solve problems as they arise. Encourage or require teams of teachers (or teachers and administrators) to attend the same inservice programs so that whole groups of teachers have similar orientations and experiences.

6. Provide leadership in making teachers comfortable in their roles as experimenters, risk takers, and team players. Provide support for alternative teaching strategies, give encouragement rather than criticism when activities fail, and make time for educators to meet in groups to develop cooperative and team efforts.

STATE ROLES

1. Make routine budget allocations and press for additional funds for staff development to support good science teaching. Pay special attention to the training of those responsible for science education in districts, with the expectation that they will create similar opportunities for their teachers and administrators.

2. Communicate with local administrators and others responsible for science education about the availability of federal funds that are allocated exclusively to improve K-12 science and mathematics teaching. Encourage local educators to use these pass-through monies in ways that will enhance psychological, material, and structural supports for teachers.

3. Ensure that all state frameworks and guidelines justify and support constructivist science as described in this book. It is often more convincing when classroom or district personnel can cite an authoritative source to justify a particular approach to teaching.

4. Develop and support regional science education networks within your state where teachers and others can periodically gather to discuss problems and new strategies. Select topics of particular interest to elementary teachers, such as innovative curriculum materials or understanding space probes.

5. Explore networking via electronic communication. With only a few current uses around the country, electronic communication holds promise for the future. The McGraw-Hill MIX system, for example, is popular with some states already developing statewide or regional bulletin boards.

6. Create and present awards in a meaningful ceremony for exemplary science teaching at the elementary level, much as the Presidential Awards competition does. In some states, the governor, the state commissioner of education, or the state board of education recognizes exemplary teachers. The National Science Foundation is awarding grants to K-12 teachers in each state for excellence and leadership in mathematics and science. State science personnel usually administer this program, with a substantial monetary award given to the finalist in each state. Consider developing a similar state program.

7. Work with appropriate legislative bodies to pass legislation that affirms the need and value of elementary school science programs. Included in such legislation could be provisions for curriculum improvement, staff development, and release time for teachers and others to work together for self- and school improvement.

8. Disseminate media releases that reaffirm the research that thinking, reasoning teachers planning together provide a statewide basis for improving schools. Highlight efforts in which teachers are involved in meaningful ways to improve science programs in their buildings and districts. Focus attention on instances in which teachers share leadership in their schools and where science is a priority.

MODELS AND RESOURCES

A Resource Guide: *Science for Children: Resources for Teachers* is a publication of the National Science Resources Center (NSRC). The guide lists curriculum materials, supplementary materials, and sources of information and assistance that can be very helpful in supporting a constructivist-oriented science program. The NSRC also sponsors summer institutes for school district elementary science leadership teams.

A Source of Exemplary Programs: The National Science Teachers Association's Search for Excellence in Science Education Program has identified districts where strong teacher development and support systems are leading to effective science education in elementary schools. Descriptions of these programs are published periodically in the NSTA's (1985, 1988) Focus on Excellence Series. Examples of several support efforts are described below.

A Source of Exemplary Programs: The National Diffusion Network disseminates several exemplary elementary science programs, each with its own materials and teacher training and support components. Programs that support constructivist science include Conservation for Children (San Jose, California); Hands-On Elementary Science (Frederick, Maryland); Life Lab Science Program (Capitola, California); Marine Science Project: FOR SEA (Poulsbo, Washington); and STARWALK (Peoria, Illinois). (See Lewis 1988 for more on these innovative programs.)

A Resource for Principals: The National Science Teachers Association, with funding from NSF, is sponsoring a number of Regional Science Leadership centers across the country to support principals as leaders for science education. The PAL centers conduct two-day training sessions in which principals can learn about hands-on science, receive materials, and prepare to train and support teachers within their schools. The project, directed by Ken Mechling and Donna Oliver (1983), is located at Clarion State University in Pennsylvania.

A Material Support System Model: The elementary science program in Carroll County, Maryland, has a unique materials support model. Each spring, Carroll County teachers receive an order packet for science materials. The packet is set up as an inventory control vehicle for the kits, which house all the necessary materials for curriculum activities. (Early in the program, the science supervisor shopped for necessary curriculum materials. The contents of the Carroll County materials kits are now provided by a commercial vendor.) Principals have the responsibility of providing appropriate amounts of the cost-per-student allotment for science. If teachers do not have the necessary materials, the science supervisor is informed. Live materials for activities are provided in house. A high school science teacher works part time with student aides to maintain cultures and live specimens, providing them to elementary teachers as needed.

A Material Support System Model: In Anchorage, Alaska, more than 1,000 teachers in 55 schools get needed supplies for science from a central system that manages purchasing and dissemination of equipment and material supplies. Materials are circulated to teachers on a prearranged schedule. Early in the school year, teachers complete a form that alerts the science center to their needs. Teachers teach at least four science units a year—one hour a day, three days a week. Teachers are encouraged to use additional resources and develop interdisciplinary connections to the science unit. The materials for each unit are assembled into a kit at the science center and then delivered to the teachers as scheduled. The kits remain with each teacher for six weeks.

The center's staff orders and stores all materials needed to teach the units, assembles class-sized sets of materials; maintains a truck delivery route so that teachers receive materials when they need them; and inventories, cleans, and replenishes all materials when they are returned. This cost-effective sharing system allows for a wider range of units to be taught. Moreover, duplication of costly materials can be kept to a minimum. Another plus is that the science center serves as a concrete focal point for the elementary science program. Teachers, administrators, and the community have become aware of the strong science program in place and how it facilitates good science teaching.

A Material Support System Model: An example of a support system for teachers in a small, rural school is Westford Elementary School in northwestern Vermont. Two summers ago, the Parent Teachers Group (PTG) donated $2,000 to purchase supplies for the elementary science program. A committee of parents and teachers worked together to select and order basic materials for the classrooms. The principal offered support by locating a small, centrally located utility space to house the materials. Other townspeople helped by donating storage shelves for the space and by purchasing and labeling storage containers for the new materials.

The teachers use a simple sign-out system to keep track of the equipment. Volunteers inventory and help with the upkeep of the storage area. This year the PTG again donated money. Additional supplies, as well as science resource materials that will support teachers in implementing their newly adopted science curriculum, are being purchased. This is one example of science being widely supported in a small community.

An Association for Science Leaders: The Leadership Institute for Science Education (LISE) Center is a professional development and resource center of the National Science Supervisors Association (NSSA). Through a national cadre of trained science leaders, the LISE Center provides programs and resources to promote leadership development and teacher advocacy for science education. Among its services are institutes, conferences, seminars, and leadership publications.

Institutes for Science Leadership: The National Science Resources Center (NSRC) has a program of summer Elementary Science Leadership Institutes that prepare leadership teams—teachers, science supervisors, school system administrators, and scientists—to organize elementary science program improvement efforts for their local school districts.

A Model for Teachers Supporting Teachers: The PACT Program in Jefferson County Schools, Colorado, places teachers in the roles of university clinical faculty, mentors for beginning teachers, and instructors for district inservice activities. Exemplary classroom teachers are chosen by Metro State College, the University of Colorado at Denver, and the Jeffco School District for a one-year leave of absence. During that time, PACT teachers teach at the university and mentor two preservice teachers. They also conduct district inservices and consult with principals about curriculum and instructional issues.

Key References

Darling-Hammond, L. (1986). *A Conceptual Framework for Examining and Staffing Schooling*. Santa Monica, Calif.: RAND Corporation.

Hord, S. M., W. L. Rutherford, L. Huling-Austin, and G. E. Hall. (1987). *Taking Charge of Change*. Alexandria, Va.: ASCD.

Lewis, M. G. (1988). *Science Education Programs that Work*. Washington, D.C.: National Diffusion Network, Office of Educational Research and Improvement, U.S. Department of Education.

Lightfoot, S. L. (1983). *The Good High School: Portraits of Character and Culture*. New York: Basic Books.

Loucks-Horsley, S., M. Carlson, L. Brink, P. Horwitz, D. Marsh, H. Pratt, and K. Worth. (1989). *Developing and Supporting Teachers for Elementary School Science Education*. Andover, Mass.: The National Center for Improving Science Education, The NETWORK, Inc.

Loucks-Horsley, S., and L. F. Hergert. (1985). *An Action Guide to School Improvement*. Andover, Mass.: The NETWORK, Inc., and Alexandria, Va.: ASCD.

McLaughlin, M. W. (1987). "Learning from Experience: Lessons from Policy Implementation." *Educational Evaluation and Policy Analysis 9*, 2: 171-8.

Mechling, K. R., and D. L. Oliver. (1983). *Promoting Science Among Elementary School Principals*. Washington, D.C.: National Science Teachers Association.

National Science Resources Center. (1989). *Science for Children: Resources for Teachers*. Washington, D.C.: NSRC.

National Science Teachers Association. (1985). *Focus on Excellence Series*. Elementary: 1:2. Washington, D.C.: NSTA.

National Science Teachers Association. (1988). *Focus on Excellence Series*. Elementary: 4:3. Washington, D.C.: NSTA.

Odden, A., and D. Marsh. (April 1988). "How Comprehensive Reform Legislation Can Improve Secondary Schools." *Phi Delta Kappan 69*: 593-598.

Weiss, I. S. (1987). *Report of the 1985-1986 National Survey of Science and Mathematics Education*. Washington, D.C.: National Science Foundation.

Appendix A
General Reference List for Science Leaders

American Association for the Advancement of Science. (1989). *Project 2061: Science for All Americans*. Washington, D.C.: AAAS.

Bybee, R. W., C. E. Buchwald, L. S. Crissman, D. Heil, P. J. Kuerbis, C. Matsumoto, and J. D. McInerney. (1989). *Science and Technology Education for the Elementary Years: Frameworks for Curriculum and Instruction*. Andover, Mass.: The National Center for Improving Science Education, The NETWORK, Inc.

Champagne, A. B., ed. (1988). *This Year in School Science 1988: Science Teaching: Making the System Work*. Washington, D.C.: American Association for the Advancement of Science.

Champagne, A. B., B. E. Lovitts, and B. J. Calinger, eds. (1989). *This Year in School Science 1989: Scientific Literacy*. Washington, D.C.: American Association for the Advancement of Science.

Cole, M. and P. Griffin. (1987). *Improving Science and Mathematics Education for Minorities and Women: Contextual Factors in Education*. Madison: Wisconsin Center for Education Research, School of Education.

Driver, R., E. Guesne, and A. Tiberghien. (1985). *Children's Ideas in Science*. Great Britain: Open University Press.

Harlen, W. (1985). *Teaching and Learning Primary Science*. New York: Teachers College Press, Columbia University.

Hord, S. M, W. L. Rutherford, L. Huling-Austin, and G. E. Hall. (1987). *Taking Charge of Change*. Alexandria, Va.: Association for Supervision and Curriculum Development.

International Association for the Evaluation of Educational Achievement. (1988). *Science Achievement in Seventeen Countries. A Preliminary Report*. Elmsford, N.Y.: Pergamon Press.

LaPointe, A. E., N. A. Mead, and G. W. Phillips. (1989). *A World of Differences: An International Assessment of Mathematics and Science*. Princeton, N.J.: Educational Testing Service.

Loucks-Horsley, S., and L. F. Hergert. (1985). *An Action Guide to School Improvement*. Andover, Mass.: The NETWORK, Inc. and Alexandria, Va.: Association for Supervision and Curriculum Development.

Loucks-Horsley, S., C. K. Harding, M. A. Arbuckle, L. B. Murray, C. Dubea, and M. K. Williams. (1987). *Continuing to Learn: A Guidebook for Teacher Development*. Andover, Mass.: The Regional Laboratory for Educational Improvement of the Northeast and Islands.

Loucks-Horsley, S., M. O. Carlson, L. Brink, P. Horwitz, D. Marsh, H. Pratt, and K. Worth. (1989). *Developing and Supporting Teachers for Elementary School Science Education*. Andover, Mass.: The National Center for Improving Science Education, The NETWORK, Inc.

Motz, L. L., and G. M. Madrazo, Jr., eds. (1988). *Third Sourcebook for Science Supervisors*. Washington, D.C.: National Science Teachers Association.

Mullis, I. V. S., and L. B. Jenkins. (1988). *The Science Report Card: Elements of Risk and Recovery*. Princeton, N.J.: Educational Testing Service.

Murnane, R. J., and S. A. Raizen. (1988). *Improving Indicators of the Quality of Science and Mathematics Education in Grades K-12*. Washington, D.C.: National Academy Press.

National Center for Improving Science Education. (1989). *Getting Started in Science: A Blueprint for Elementary School Science Education.* Andover, Mass.: The National Center for Improving Science Education, The NETWORK, Inc.

National Science Resources Center. (1988). *Science for Children: Resources for Teachers*. Washington, D.C.: National Academy Press.

Raizen, S. A., J. B. Baron, A. B. Champagne, E. Haertel, I. V. S. Mullis, and J. Oakes. (1989). *Assessment in Elementary School Science Education*. Andover, Mass.: The National Center for Improving Science Education, The NETWORK, Inc.

Resnick, L. B. (1987). *Education and Learning to Think*. Washington, D.C.: National Academy Press.

Weiss, I. S. (1987). *Report of the 1985-86 National Survey of Science and Mathematics Education*. Washington, D.C.: National Science Foundation.

Appendix B
Science Resources

American Association for the Advancement of Science (AAAS)
1333 H St., N.W.
Washington, D.C. 20005
(F. James Rutherford, Chief Education Officer and Project 2061 Director)

Anchorage School District
P.O. Box 196614
Anchorage, AK 99519-6614
(Emma Walton, Science Coordinator)

Association for Constructivist Teaching
Prentice Rd.
Worthington, MA 01098
(Catherine Fosnot, President)

Biological Sciences Curriculum Study (BSCS)
830 N. Tejon, Suite 405
Colorado Springs, CO 80903
(Rodger W. Bybee, Principal Investigator, Science for Life and Living)

California State Department of Education
Publications
P.O. Box 271
Sacramento, CA 95802-0271

Carleton College
Department of Geology
One N. College St.
Northfield, MN 55057
(Ed Buchwald, Professor)

Carrol County Public Schools
55 N. Court St.
Westminster, MD 21157
(Gary E. Dunkleberger and Brian L. Lockard)

CD-ROM Science Helper
University of Florida
Room 302, Norman Hall
Gainesville, FL 32607
(Mary Budd Rowe, Project Director)

Connecticut Department of Education
P.O. Box 2219
Hartford, CT 06145
(Joan B. Baron, Director of Program Evaluation)

Conservation for Children
John Muir Elementary School
6560 Hanover Dr.
San Jose, CA 95129
(Marilyn Bodourian, Project Director)

Denver Audubon Society Urban Education Dissemination Project
975 Grant St.
Denver, CO 80203
(Karen Hollweg, Project Director)

Department of Education and Science and the Welsh Office
National Curriculum Council
Room G-1
45 Notting Hill Gate
London, W 113 JB England

Education Development Center (EDC)
55 Chapel St.
Newton, MA 02160
(Karen Worth, Judith Sandler, Principal Investigators, Improving Urban Elementary Science)

Florida Department of Education
444 FEC
Tallahassee, FL 32399
(Jack Hopper, Elementary Science Consultant)

Full Option Science System
Center for Multisensory Learning
Lawrence Hall of Science
University of California
Berkeley, CA 94720
(Lawrence F. Lowery, Project
    Director)

Hands-On Elementary Science
Education Department
Hood College
Frederick, MD 21701
(Dean A. Wood, Project Director)

**Humanities and Technology
    Association**
Department of Technology
Northern Kentucky University
Nun Dr.
Highland Heights, KY 41076
(James Gray, Editor)

**Indiana Department of
    Education**
Room 229 Statehouse
Indianapolis, IN 46204
(Jerry Colglazie, Science
    Coordinator)

Invent America!
United States Patent Model
    Foundation
Courthouse Square
510 King St.
Alexandria, VA 22134

Jefferson County School District
1829 Denver West Dr.
Bldg. 27
Golden, CO 80401
(Harold Pratt, Executive Director
    for Science and Technology;
    Susan Shiff, Staff Development
    Academy)

**Leadership Institute for Science
    Education (LISE) Center**
Copernicus Hall, Room 227
Central Connecticut State
    University
1615 Stanley St.
New Britain, CT 06050
(Kenneth Russell Roy, National
    Director)

Life Lab
1156 High St.
Santa Cruz, CA 95064
(Roberta M. Jaffe, Lisa Glick, Gary
    Appel, Project Directors)

Marine Science Project: FOR SEA
Marine Science Center
17771 Fjord Dr., N.E.
Poulsbo, WA 98370
(Laurie Dumdie, Project Director)

Mesa School District
Science Resource Center
143 Alma School Rd.
Mesa, AR 85202
(Susan Sprague, Joanne Wolfe)

**Metropolitan Toronto School
    Board**
45 York Mills Rd.
Willowdale, Ontario M2P 1B6
Canada

**Michigan State Department of
    Education**
P.O. Box 30008
Lansing, MI 48909
(Mozell Lang, Science Specialist)

Michigan State University
Department of Teacher Education
Erickson Hall
College of Education
E. Lansing, MI 48824

Minneapolis Public Schools
801 Broadway, N.E.
Minneapolis, MN 55413
(Joseph A. Premo, Science
    Consultant)

**Mt. Diablo Unified School
    District**
1936 Carlotta Dr.
Concord, CA 94519

**National Association for
    Science, Technology, and
    Society (NASTS)**
Pennsylvania State University
117 Willard Bldg.
University Park, PA 16802

National Astrophysics Center
Harvard University
60 Garden St.
Cambridge, MA 02138

National Diffusion Network
Office of Educational Research
and Improvement
US Department of Education
555 New Jersey Ave., N.W.
Washington, DC 20208-1525

**National School Boards
Association**
1680 Duke St.
Alexandria, VA 22314
(Adria Thomas, Director of
Research and Information
Services)

**National Science Resources
Center**
Arts and Industries Bldg., Room
1201
Smithsonian Institution
Washington, DC 20560
(Douglas Lapp, Executive
Director; Joe H. Griffith, Project
Director, Science and
Technology for Children)

**National Science Teachers
Association**
1742 Connecticut Ave., N.W.
Washington, DC 20009

**New York State Department of
Education**
Washington Ave.
Albany, NY 12234
(Douglas S. Reynolds, Chief,
Bureau of Science Education)

**Oregon State Department of
Education**
700 Pringle Pkwy., S.E.
Salem, OR 97310
(Raymond E. Thiess, Specialist,
Science Education)

PAL Project
Clarion State University
Peirce Science Center, B-45
Clarion, PA 16264
(Ken Mechling and Donna
Oliver, Project Directors)

Pittsburgh Public Schools
341 S. Bellefield Ave.
Pittsburgh, PA 15213

**Pittsburgh Regional Center for
Science Teachers**
Carnegie Institute
4400 Forbes Ave.
Pittsburgh, PA 15213
(Jane Conrad)

Purdue University
School Mathematics and Science
Center
W. Lafayette, IN 47907
(William C. Kyle, Jr.)

Pyramid Films and Media, Inc.
114 W. Front St.
Media, PA 19063

**The Regional Laboratory for
Educational Improvement of
the Northeast and Islands**
Center for Teaching Thinking
300 Brickstone Sq., Suite 900
Andover, MA 01810
(Jill Mirman Owen, Robert
Swartz, Directors)

**Roundout Valley Central School
District**
Box 9
Accord, NY 12404
(James Vertucci, Director of
Instruction)

**Science through Science,
Technology, and Society
(S-STS) Group**
Pennsylvania State University
117 Willard Bldg.
University Park, PA 16802

Schaumburg Science Program
District 54 Elementary Schools
Schaumburg, IL 60172
(Larry Small)

Shoreham-Wading River Central School District
Shoreham, NY 11786-9745
(Martin Brooks, Assistant
Superintendent)

STARWALK
Lakeview Museum Planetarium
1125 W. Lake Ave.
Peoria, IL 61614

Teacher's Clearinghouse for Science, Technology, and Society
The New Walden Lincoln School
One W. 88th St.
New York, NY 10024

Technical Education Research Centers, Inc.
1696 Massachusetts Ave.
Cambridge, MA 02138
(Robert Tinker, Project Director,
Kids Network)

Tennessee State Department of Education
214 Cordell Hull Bldg.
Nashville, TN 37219
(Geraldine Farmer, State Science
Consultant)

University of New Hampshire
Department of Education
105-B Morrill Hall
Durham, NH 03824
(Sharon Oja, Professor)

University of Northern Colorado
Science and Mathematics for
Elementary Preservice Teachers
Rose Hall/Mass. Department
Greeley, CO 80639
(Henry Heikkinen, Director)

University of the State of New York
State Education Department
Publications Sales Desk
Room 171, Education Bldg.
Addition
Albany, NY 12234

University of Wyoming
Wyoming Center for Teaching
and Learning
Box 3992
Room 406, Wyoming Hall
University Station
Laramie, WY 82071
(Vince Sindt, Director; Peter
Ellsworth, Coordinator)

Urban Coalition
8601 Georgia Ave., Room 500
Silver Spring, MD 20910

Virginia Department of Education
P.O. Box 6Q
Richmond, VA 23216
(Joseph D. Exline, Associate
Director for Science)

Westford Elementary School
Brookside
Westford, VT 05494
(Maura Carlson)

Weston Public Schools
444 Wellesley St.
Weston, MA 02193

Wisconsin Department of Public Instruction
Publications Department
P.O. Box 7841
Madison, WI 53702-7841

About the Authors

Susan Loucks-Horsley is Associate Director of the National Center for Improving Science Education at The NETWORK, Inc., in Andover, Massachusetts, where she is responsible for the Center's work in teacher development and support and for publications for practitioners. She is also Program Director of The Regional Laboratory for Educational Improvement of the Northeast and Islands, where she develops materials and programs to improve staff development in schools and districts. A co-developer of the Concerns-Based Adoption Model while at the Texas Research and Development Center for Teacher Education, she is widely published in the areas of educational change and school improvement, as well as staff development.

Roxanne Kapitan is Communication Specialist for the National Center for Improving Science Education at The NETWORK, Inc., in Andover, Massachusetts, where she writes publications for practitioner audiences. She is also Director of NutriWork, a program promoting good nutrition through the workplace. She has been involved in many curriculum development projects and is currently working with the American Cancer Society on a K-12 nutrition intervention program entitled Changing the Course. She also provides training for nutrition and health education professionals in the areas of program effectiveness and marketing.

Maura O'Brien Carlson is Research Associate for the National Center for Improving Science Education at The NETWORK, Inc., in Burlington, Vermont, where she has worked in the areas of teacher preparation and support for elementary science. She is currently starting the Vermont Elementary Science Project, applying the recommendations of the Center to elementary science programs in several districts in Vermont. She has worked as an adjunct instructor at the University of Vermont, teaching elementary science methods, and has developed teacher training programs for inservice teachers in science education.

Paul J. Kuerbis is Project Director of Curriculum and Instruction for the National Center for Improving Science Education at the Biological Sciences Curriculum Study (BSCS) in Colorado Springs, Colorado, and Associate Professor of Education at Colorado College. His primary work with the National Center is in the area of science curriculum and instruction. A teacher educator at Colorado College, his major interest is in the preparation and inservice development of science teachers, particularly in the area of instruction. He has also worked extensively with BSCS on the development of curriculums for elementary and middle school students.

Richard C. Clark is Science Specialist for the Minnesota State Department of Education, a position he has held for the last 20 years. Working extensively with K-12 science teachers, he is particularly interested in establishing networking systems that bring together isolated teachers. He has developed several state frameworks and guides for teachers in Minnesota and has served as President of the National Science Supervisors Association and the Council of State Science Supervisors.

G. Marge Melle recently retired as Coordinator of Early Childhood Education for the Jefferson County Schools in Golden, Colorado. There she coordinated the development of the Primary Integrated Curriculum (PIC), an integration of science and technology, social studies, career, health, and environmental education for primary grades. She currently is a national consultant on science staff development, integrated program development, and cooperative learning, while also teaching science to 3rd and 4th graders.

Thomas P. Sachse is Manager of Math, Science, and Environmental Education for the California Department of Education. He has coordinated the development of science and environmental education curriculum guides for the state of California and works actively in reforming instructional materials and testing programs. He advocates the implementation of quality science and technology programs at the national, state, and local levels.

Emma Walton is Science Coordinator for the Anchorage, Alaska, School District. She was President of the National Association of Science Supervisors in 1988-89 and is currently Divisional Director for Supervision of the National Science Teachers Association. As a local science coordinator, she has been on the cutting edge of developing and implementing hands-on/minds-on science programs, including one recognized as exemplary by the National Science Teachers Association. She is the author of numerous papers and articles and has made presentations locally, nationally, and internationally.